Assessing the gender impact of development projects

Royal Tropical Institute
KIT Press
Mauritskade 63
1092 AD Amsterdam
The Netherlands
(20)-5688272

ETC International BV
Kastanjelaan 5
P.O. Box 64
3830 AB Leusden
The Netherlands
(33)-943086

Intermediate Technology
Publications
103-105 Southampton Row
London WC1B 4HH
United Kingdom
(171)-4369761

Published in 1994 in the UK by Intermediate Technology Publications,
103-105 Southampton Row, London WC1B 4HH, United Kingdom
United Kingdom ISBN 1 85339 271 5
A CIP catalogue record for this book is available from the British Library

CIP-DATA KONINKLIJKE BIBLIOTHEEK, DEN HAAG

Assessing the gender impact of development projects : case studies from Bolivia,
Burkina Faso and India / Vera Gianotten...[et al.]. - Amsterdam :
Royal Tropical Institute. - Ill., photos
With ref.
ISBN 90-6832-707-0
NUGI 661
Subject heading: women and development projects.

© 1994 Directorate General for International Cooperation
Ministry of Foreign Affairs, The Hague
Production and distribution: Royal Tropical Institute, Amsterdam
Cover design: Nel Punt, Amsterdam
Translation and editing: A. van Blaaderen-Thistleton
Printing: ICG Printing, Dordrecht
ISBN 90 6832 707 0

Cover:
Bolivia: Andean women ploughing: their productive activities are just as important to the rural
economy as those of men
Photo: KIT Photobureau
Burkina Faso: Making an activity profile with a couple, using 'genderless' drawings of productive
and reproductive tasks carried out in the household and community
Photo: Margriet Reinders
India: Transect of borewell irrigation scheme in Burgula village, by women of the households who
own the fields; men are kept aside by male team members
Photo: Annet Lingen

Assessing the gender impact of development projects

Vera Gianotten

Verona Groverman

Edith van Walsum

Lida Zuidberg

Case studies from Bolivia, Burkina Faso and India

Royal Tropical Institute – The Netherlands

ETC International BV – The Netherlands

Intermediate Technology – United Kingdom

Table of contents

Abbreviations

APLIFT	Andhra Pradesh Surface Water Lift Irrigation Schemes
APSIDC	Andhra Pradesh State Irrigation Development Corporation
APWELL	Andhra Pradesh Groundwater Borewell Irrigation Schemes
BPAF	Bureau de Promotion des Activités Féminines *(Office for the Promotion of Women's Interests)*
CNPAR	Centre National de Promotion des Artisans Ruraux *(National Centre for the Promotion of Rural Artisans)*
CORDECH	Corporación de Desarrollo Regional de Chuquisaca *(Regional Development Corporation of Chuquisaca)*
CRPA	Centre Régional de Promotion Agro-pastorale *(Regional Centre for Agro-pastoral Promotion)*
DAC	Development Assistance Committee of the OECD
DGIS	Directoraat Generaal Internationale Samenwerking *(Directorate General for International Cooperation of the Dutch Ministry of Foreign Affairs)*
DRET	Direction Régionale de l'Environnement et du Tourisme *(Regional Department of the Environment and Tourism)*
DROMR	Direction Régionale de l'Organisation du Monde Rural *(Regional Department for Community Development)*
DRPC	Direction Régionale du Plan et de Coopération *(Regional Department of Planning and Cooperation)*
IMF	International Monetary Fund
IRDAS	Institute of Resource Development and Social Management
LIS	Lift Irrigation Scheme
NGO	Non-Governmental Organization
OECD	Organization for Economic Cooperation and Development
PDISAB	Programme de Développement Intégré dans les provinces du Sanguié et du Boulkiemdé *(Integrated Development Programme in Sanguié and Boulkiemdé Provinces)*
PROGRESS	People's Research Organization for Grass-root Environmental Scientific Service
RRA	Rapid Rural Appraisal

Acknowledgements

The authors are grateful for the openness and cooperation of all organizations and individuals involved in the gender assessment studies, that form the basis and primary input for this book.

In Bolivia, it would have been impossible to carry out the study without the commitment of all the women and men of the peasant communities of Pucará, Qewiñas, Fuerte Rua and Otorongo. During the field study, the researchers enjoyed the excellent cooperation of the staff and members of CARE and the regional development corporation CORDECH. The author is further very grateful to the Bolivian consultants Evelyn Barrón and Felipa Aguilar, who played a crucial role in the data collection. Special thanks are also directed to Ana Rochkovski, Women and Development specialist of the Netherlands Office of Development Cooperation in La Paz, for her conceptual and logistical support.

The Burkina Faso study was made possible by the contributions of the local consultant, Kadidia Tall, who was also responsible for the pre-study. Secondly, the cooperation of the organizations involved in project implementation, in particular the staff of the Regional Department of Planning and Cooperation, members of the Interprovincial Committee of the project, the project management committee and the technical assistants was indispensable. Thirdly, the field team, composed of two local consultants and four field assistants, guaranteed consistency in data collection during the field study. The heartfelt cooperation of the population of the six research villages made the field study an exciting experience. Last but not least, the Royal Netherlands Embassy in Ouagadougou must be mentioned with respect to the support given during the initiation, execution and follow-up of the study.

In India, special words of thanks must be given to the Indian consultancy group 'Think Soft', who participated in the preparations and implementation of the study, and ETC India, for their involvement. Special thanks are also due the staff of APSIDC, who accommodated the study in a very cooperative way. The open discussions of the study team with staff of the NGOs concerned and with the village women and men are reflected in the results of the study and are highly appreciated. The Netherlands Embassy in India is also thanked for their organizational and conceptual support.

In the Netherlands, the authors would like to Annet Lingen, Joan Boer and Els Klinkert, who gave support during the implementation of the study and the writing of this book. Special thanks also go to KIT Press and to Anne van Blaaderen-Thistleton, for her work in translating and editing.

Finally, the authors are grateful to the Directorate General for International Cooperation of the Netherlands Ministry of Foreign Affairs, whose financial support helped to make publication possible.

Vera Gianotten
Verona Groverman
Edith van Walsum
Lida Zuidberg

Preface

Gender analysis can and should play a role in furthering the efficiency and effectiveness of development projects. The gender assessment studies presented here, which I am honoured to introduce, underline the importance of early gender analysis. The authors have tested an analytical framework developed by our staff, using it (in close collaboration with the staff) to investigate the role of gender analysis in three settings. The results showed, among other things, the extent to which project proposals can suffer from erroneous assumptions. One striking example was found in the Andes, where it had been routinely supposed that gathering firewood would be a concern of women – while in reality, in this region, this is a task of men.

The need to develop a methodology for gender assessment to be used at a very early stage of project preparation became more urgent after the introduction, in 1991, of a procedure to screen all project proposals with respect to their possible effects on poverty, women and environment. At that point, much experience with environmental impact studies was already available. In the areas of poverty and of gender, however, there was still a distinct lack of tools that could be used systematically to assemble the appropriate baseline data and to predict the likely consequences of a proposed activity. Our Ministry felt keenly that this imbalance needed to be redressed as soon as possible. Workers in the field added to the pressure, making increasingly strong demands for tools to be used in translating policies on women and development and gender into practice.

Clearly, these policies – as a integral part of development thinking – are still relatively new, even though, since the early nineteen-seventies, much of the groundwork has been laid. Important concepts have been evolved, case material has been accumulated, strategies have been laid down and people at all levels have been confronted with the relevance of gender-sensitive approaches. But the threshold of full-scale operational application will remain difficult to cross until our attitudes change.

Attitudes towards the role of women are, after all, deeply rooted in all cultures, whether in the developing world or elsewhere. The straightforward fact that women can make an equal contribution to the development process, and that they should be entitled and enabled to do so, is not always readily understood. Perhaps the material presented in these studies will help to make women's roles less of a blind spot.

The research reported here resulted initially in the *Gender Assessment Study* publication that serves as a methodological guideline for our Ministry. This book is addressed to a wider audience, and expands on that study, both by adding to the analytical framework and by including suggestions for its applicability. I am pleased with this further step towards making gender policy operational, and I hope many readers will become enthusiastic users. In the end, it is women who will gain from such efforts; through them, development will also benefit.

Gertjan Storm
Acting Director General for International Cooperation
The Netherlands

The Hague, October 1994

Introduction

Will proposed development projects have the effects intended? Who will benefit, and who will not? What side-effects are likely? These are the kinds of questions behind the methodology discussed here: 'gender assessment studies' can serve as planning instruments that can help to achieve the desired effects for women, leading to improvements in their position and prospects in life.

A wide range of development projects and programmes involving women have been implemented in recent decades, and many studies have been made of women's situation and position in society. Development models have gradually come to perceive women as active actors instead of victims and passive objects, and various approaches to women and development have been applied. We have gradually come to realize that, if projects are to improve women's position, it is essential to have the different needs and interests of women and men, and the power relations between them, taken into account in the planning phase. This suggests a need for attention to 'gender' – 'women's and men's socially defined roles and characteristics, which are shaped by historical, economic, religious, cultural and ethnic factors.' Using the term gender underlines the fact that women's position is not so much a result of biological differences between women and men, but rather of socially determined gender differences. (Lingen, 1994)

Development projects can have either positive or negative effects on the division of labour, and the access to and control over allocation of resources, benefits, and decision-making in a society. When gender differences are overlooked in the planning phase, projects are unlikely to respond to women's needs and may even have negative consequences for women. Moreover, it must be recognized that different groups of women (farmers and non-farmers, rich and poor, and so forth) have different interests; and that the interests of women cited in a proposed project or programme must be reflected in the design of activities and institutional linkages, so that intentions become reality.

The realization of the necessity for a more focused look at project design has been the product of many debates on theory and practice. The early phases of development cooperation in the 1950s and 1960s saw the application of a welfare approach, which viewed women as purely passive beneficiaries in the development process, emphasizing their reproductive role. The anti-poverty approach of the 1970s was related to the basic needs strategy. While this approach recognized that women had an important role to play in meeting basic needs, it was mainly limited to one of producers in the context of self-sufficiency. After 1980 a third, 'women in development' approach emerged, which acknowledged the importance of integrating women into the development process to strengthen the national economy. The underlying assumption was that integrating women into the development process would make it more efficient and effective. This approach was based upon the (mistaken) premise that women were not yet 'integrated' and that women's work had not yet contributed to national development.

All three approaches overlooked historically-based inequalities of power between men and women, in the economic as well as social and personal spheres (Lycklama à Nijeholt, 1987; DGIS, 1990). In reaction, the 'autonomy' and 'empowerment' approaches emerged, based on the view that structural inequality between the sexes can be overcome by strengthening and broadening women's power base (DGIS, 1992; Moser, 1993).

In 1990, in the policy document *A world of difference* (DGIS, 1990), the Directorate General for International Cooperation (DGIS) of the Netherlands' Ministry of Foreign Affairs discussed the need for implementing certain activities prior to projects: first, collection of baseline data (such as national gender profiles); and second, a screening with respect to potential effects (or 'impact' – as in the already well-known 'environmental impact reports'). This, in conjunction with the evolution of the concepts of autonomy and empowerment of women, suggested the development of a methodology, which could serve as a planning instrument and also perhaps give an indication of the potential impact of proposed development projects and programmes on gender relations.

In addition, criteria for projects were developed (based on the DAC/WID[1] procedural criteria), including the involvement of women in design and implementation, the alleviation of constraints to the participation of women, and the incorporation of gender expertise. These criteria are intended to guarantee both the target group's participation, and an input of women and development expertise, in the various phases of a project cycle. Often, though, the information given by project proposals on gender relations is incomplete, and gender concerns are not sufficiently incorporated in project planning. An instrument is needed that will allow examining project designs, to assure that they pay more and better attention to gender, and to allow the assessment of the impact of development projects and programmes on gender relations in a particular geographic region or specific cultural setting. DGIS therefore decided to develop a procedure for gender assessment studies, to facilitate the integration of gender issues throughout the project cycle. The task of such studies is to describe the existing position of women and to forecast the possible consequences for them of proposed interventions. The pilot phase, including the three gender assessment case studies presented in this book, were implemented by DGIS as a step toward the development of workable guidelines.

Purpose of pilot studies and the book

A preliminary methodological framework was established in accordance with the objectives of a gender assessment study (described in the following section). The purpose of the pilot studies was to test that framework, and to provide information and recommendations for designing projects that will optimally strengthen women's position. These studies served as an input for the elaboration of guidelines for gender assessment studies (Lingen, 1994), primarily for DGIS policy staff.

The pilot studies are presented here because, first, they show the importance of an in-depth analysis of gender relations during the planning phase, as a means of achieving project design and implementation that give due consideration to the needs and interests of men and women. The three studies took place in three different cultural and socioeconomic settings, and present interesting data on women's position and gender relations. They highlight the importance of making interrelated analyses of the national context; the actual position of various groups of women at local level; institutional policy and institutional strengths and weaknesses regarding gender; and the project proposal. Second, although detailed methodological recommendations for improving a gender assessment study will not be presented here,[2] the pilot studies provide insight into the general methodological framework and its strengths and weaknesses.

This book is meant primarily for persons interested in policy on women and development, and in the methodology of gender assessment studies. It is also intended for those interested in improvements to women's position, and to gender relations, in the specific context of planning and implementing development projects.

Objectives and characteristics of a gender assessment study[3]

A gender assessment study investigates a development project's expected impact on women as compared to men; it also assesses the extent to which the project responds to the specific interests and needs of different categories of women. The objectives are:
- to gain insight into relevant gender relations in the project area and women's perception of the proposed interventions;
- to gain insight into whether the institutions involved have the capacity to deal with gender issues in project planning and implementation;
- to assess from a gender perspective the possible impact of the project idea or proposal on different categories of women, and on the likely participation of women and men in various project phases;
- to formulate recommendations for further planning and monitoring of the project, so that it will optimally strengthen women's position.

A gender assessment study has several primary characteristics with respect to duration, data, focus and outcome.

Duration. An 'average' gender assessment study will take about three months. The exact duration depends on such factors as the amount of relevant data already available, the complexity of the project proposal, and the size and diversity of the project area (e.g. heterogeneity of the target group and complexity of the environment).

Data and focus. A gender assessment study uses a variety of data collection techniques, including rapid rural appraisal methods, to produce mainly qualitative data. Its strong practical orientation is meant to complement long-term scientific research. A gender assessment study should if possible take place in dialogue with women and men from the beneficiary groups, and with the organizations involved in the project. To guarantee that the information is relevant and practical for planning purposes, a gender assessment study takes the project area, sectors and implementing institutions proposed in the project documents as a starting point. It focuses on gender roles and needs primarily in relation to the identified intervention sectors.

Outcome. The assessment of ex-ante effects on women, as compared to men, is a difficult process and full of uncertainties. A gender assessment study can provide only hypotheses about a project's expected impact on the beneficiary group. Baseline data will often be incomplete, social processes do not follow strict rules and intervening factors cannot always be foreseen. Moreover, the completeness of the project document is very important: the less well defined the beneficiary groups, strategy and/or activities, the more speculative the impact assessment. This, however, only emphasizes the usefulness of gender assessment studies as planning instruments, which can help to remedy these problems before a project begins.

Pilot studies

Three projects were selected for study.[4] In addition to making a gender assessment, the researchers were responsible for giving an account of the methodological issues that had to be dealt with (see note 2). The studies took place in 1992 and 1993 and had an average duration of ten weeks.

The first study concerns the Central Chuquisaca Renewable Natural Resources Management Project (*Proyecto para el Manejo de Recursos Naturales Renovables de la Región Chuquisaca Centro*) in Bolivia. The implementing organization is CARE, a North American non-governmental organization (NGO) with offices in La Paz, Tarija and Sucre. The proposed project will be implemented by CARE-Sucre, in coordination with CORDECH *(Corporación de Desarrollo Regional de Chuquisaca),* the Regional Development Corporation of the Bolivian government. The main objective is to improve the socioeconomic position of 2,000 families in 40 peasant communities through the rational and sustainable management of natural resources. At the time of the study (July 1992) a project document was available and the project was in the appraisal phase of the DGIS approval procedures.

The second study looked at the Integrated Development Programme in Sanguié and Boulkiemdé Provinces (*Programme de Développement Intégré dans les Provinces du Sanguié et Boulkiemdé* – PDISAB) in Burkina Faso. The programme is being implemented by several government departments under the direction of the Regional department for Planning and Cooperation, with technical assistance from DGIS. The overall objectives are increased agricultural production, environmental protection and improved production conditions (health, water supply, education). At the time of the case study (October/November) the programme had been approved and had started its activities, which consisted of studies and efforts concerning collaborative planning.

In India, twin projects in Andhra Pradesh were selected: the Andhra Pradesh Surface Water Lift Irrigation Schemes (APLIFT) and the Andhra Pradesh Borewell Irrigation Schemes Projects (APWELL). The overall objectives and strategy are the same for both projects; they differ only in the irrigation output provided: borewell versus river lift irrigation schemes. Project documents were available but not yet approved, for both projects. Their main objective is to improve the living conditions of 20,000 small farmers and 13,500 marginal farmers through sustainable and environmentally sound interventions, in a way that will enable women to become equal partners of the male farmers in agricultural and other activities. The technical components of both projects will be implemented by the Andhra Pradesh State Irrigation Development Cooperation (APSIDC), while NGOs will take care of the social component.

Outline of the book

As a prelude to the three case studies, the original methodological framework and the experience gained in using it will be discussed in Chapter 1. This chapter also includes a general bibliography.

Chapter 2 presents the Bolivian case study. CARE's women and development policy is highly developed at institutional level. This is a necessary precondition. However, the overall conclusion is that further measures are needed to ensure that project interventions take women's position and gender relations in specific socioeconomic contexts into account. A general women and development policy must be supplemented with an analysis of women's role in the actual project area, to prevent wrong assumptions about that role from becoming the starting point for project interventions. For that reason, a gender assessment study can play a vital role in translating women and development policy into specific project interventions aimed at improving women's position.

The gender assessment study in Burkina Faso presented in Chapter 3 was complicated by the fact that the project plan had not been elaborated. The conclusion that the project proposal lacks a gender focus is based on its general lack of orientation regarding interventions, beneficiaries and implementation strategies. A further conclusion was that the project should take its intention 'to pay special attention to women's development' more seriously. This could be done by linking the overall and specific objectives to a more gender-sensitive approach. The results of the field study support the assertion that women's productive role must not be overlooked, which means that both male and female farmers must be explicitly included in all domains of project activities. To that end, the project activities should include gender training of decision-makers and field staff, who are often unfamiliar with the realities of peasant life.

Chapter 4 presents the gender assessment study in India, which comes to two major conclusions. First, the overall project design of both projects lacks a clear gender focus and vision of a gender-sensitive approach to be applied by the proposed implementing institutions. Secondly, the gender impact of planned project interventions depends largely on contextual variables, as described in the following chapter. Therefore it is important to take such variables into account when designing and implementing a specific intervention. The context and gender analyses carried out in four villages give insight into these variables. To strengthen the gender focus of the projects and to anticipate negative effects of planned project interventions, a gender strategy based on the outcome of these analyses is proposed. Suggestions are formulated to fit the project setting, including the institutional set-up. The project and institutional analyses provided the information necessary for making realistic suggestions.

Finally, Chapter 5 covers major findings and conclusions, the importance and limitations of a gender assessment study, and recommendations for future studies.

Notes

1. DAC/WID is the Development Assistance Committee on Women in Development of the Organization for Economic Cooperation and Development (OECD). For criteria, see OECD 1992.

2. Three specific reports were written covering the methodology of the case studies: Zuidberg and Tall (1993), Van Walsum, et al. (1993) and Gianotten et al. (1992). The final guidelines (Lingen, 1994) were based on these reports and other documentation.

3. The objectives and characteristics of a gender assessment study are from the manual based on the results of the three pilot studies (Lingen, 1994).

4. According to the selection criteria, projects had to be: at the formulation–appraisal stage or at the beginning of the implementation phase; located on different continents; and have the same (broad) sector of intervention: rural development.

Bibliography

DGIS (1990) A world of difference. A new framework for development cooperation in the 1990s. Policy document of the Directorate General for International Cooperation, Netherlands Ministry of Foreign Affairs. SDU Publishers, The Hague.

DGIS (1992) Women in development: advancing towards autonomy. The Hague.

Gianotten, V. et al. (1992) Methodologisch verslag van drie effect-studies: armoede, vrouwen en ontwikkeling, milieu. (Methodological report of three impact studies: poverty, women and development, environment.) Royal Tropical Institute (KIT), Amsterdam.

Lingen, A. (1994) Gender assessment study: a guide for policy staff. DGIS, The Hague.

Lycklama à Nijeholt G. (1987) The fallacy of integration: the UN strategy of integrating women into development revisited. Netherlands Review of Development Studies, vol. 1, pp. 57–71.

Moser C.O.N. (1993) Gender planning and development. Theory, practice and training. Routledge, London.

OECD (1992) DAC principles for effective aid, OECD publication number 43 92 06 1.

Zuidberg L. and K. Tall (1993) Methodologisch verslag van de gender impact study uitgevoerd in Burkina Faso. Ervaringen van een pilot onderzoek (Methodological report of a gender impact study in Burkina Faso. Experiences from pilot research). Royal Tropical Institute (KIT), Amsterdam.

Walsum, E. van, et al. (1993) Gender impact study in the Andhra Pradesh surface water lift irrigation schemes and borewell irrigation schemes. Report on the methodology. ETC Foundation, Leusden.

1

Methodology

A methodological framework is needed to guide a gender assesment study through its three phases: preparation (including a preparatory study), field work and reporting. The three pilot studies in the following chapters were intended to test the validity and use of the methodological framework, and to gather data that would allow the elaboration of general guidelines for policy staff regarding the implementation of gender assessment studies.

The original framework had three interrelated components: an analysis of the target group, referred to as gender analysis; an analysis of the implementing institution(s); and an analysis of the project proposal. Due to the requirements of the contract under which the case studies were carried out, the emphasis (in terms of both methodological attention and time) was on the first component: the analysis of the target group. This chapter describes how the case studies applied the framework and adapted it to the local setting. Some critical comments on the methodology are included. More detailed descriptions of the methodologies can be found in separate field reports (see note 2 in the Introduction).

A number of existing checklists and criteria were used in the analyses: the DAC/WID criteria (see Introduction) of the OECD, the *Checklist for Development Projects* (CEPAL, 1982) and the 'Key Questions' in Chapter 3 of *A Handbook for Social/Gender Analysis* (CIDA, 1989). The Harvard Analytical Framework (Overholt et al., 1985) was used for analysis of the target group. This framework is limited, however, in that it overlooks the importance of the contextual (macro) factors that influence the specific gender relations. It regards the context as an aspect of the target group analysis (gender analysis), which examines only the influencing factors derived from the micro setting. But since the contextual macrolevel factors create the setting which must be examined to understand development at microlevel, these were added as a separate component of the methodological framework.

The adapted framework served as a basis for assessing the impact of project interventions on women and gender relations. It comprised the following components: a context analysis (macrolevel); a gender analysis (microlevel); an institutional analysis; and a project analysis.

Context analysis

'Context' refers to sociocultural, economic, demographic, political and legal factors, including commercialization, macroeconomic policy, agricultural policy, legal structures, migration, etc. These macrolevel factors influence the gender relations at microlevel in various ways. Insight into these factors is needed to fully understand the situation at microlevel. For instance, changes in the food security of Indian agricultural wage labourers and their households must be seen in the context of changes in cropping patterns caused by the introduction of irrigation technology. In Bolivia, the macro-policy on food donations and food imports influences the perception of peasant women's role in the production and reproduction process. Specific examples of context analyses are found in the following chapters.

Moreover, information about general trends is an important input for the design of research questions and methods at microlevel. The Bolivia study, for example, started with an analysis of the socioeconomic and cultural aspects of Andean peasant society. This led to an emphasis in the field studies on the family and the village communal organization as the units which organize reproduction and production. The India study began with an overview of changes brought about by the modernization of agriculture regarding gender-specific access to land and other means of production, a shift to cash crops, etc. This information showed that the difference between various categories of women (and their households) was an important variable for the gender assessment. The context analysis in the Burkina Faso study was limited by lack of information on the way gender relations have changed over time. However, cultural differences between the two main ethnic groups regarding the organization of labour within the farming system, for example, were taken into account when villages were selected for field study.

Gender analysis in the research villages

As mentioned above, the macro context analysis provided the frame of reference for the gender analysis conducted at microlevel in the villages. The gender analysis gave insight into the specific effects and implications of certain developments or trends at local level, and collected information about the locality or social-specific factors.

The gender analysis examined four aspects:
- gender division of labour and workload;
- gender-related access to and control over resources and services, including benefits derived from their use;
- women's participation in decision-making and organizational capacity and, indirectly related to these, images and self-images of women;
- views and expectations of women (and men) regarding the proposed project.

Preparations for the field study

The preparatory phase consisted of a desk study of available documents regarding the project, the institutions and the characteristics of the project area. Certain 'logistical' preparations also had to be made: the selection of villages and the sectors to be covered; and the identification of categories of women and men.

The selection of research villages was complicated, in Bolivia and Burkina Faso: the institutions had not yet decided in which villages the proposed activities would be implemented. In India, however, the research villages were either already involved in an irrigation scheme or scheduled to receive irrigation.[1]

The proposed projects focused on the development of one sector: agriculture. The gender analysis, however, covered more sectors (health and nutrition for example), to make it possible to understand how the proposed interventions pertained to the realities of production and reproduction, at both household and village level.

The case studies illustrated the danger of assuming the homogeneity of a target group, not only in terms of gender but also in social–cultural terms. To gain insight into the possible impact of project interventions on people living in the project area, it is crucial to identify meaningful socioeconomic or cultural categories. As seen in the case studies, these will vary among communities. The Bolivia study took the community and the communal organizational structure as a starting point for the analysis of the households, whereas the study in Burkina Faso based the selection of households on wealth differences. In India, differentiation of socioeconomic groups was based, for example, on the capacities of households to live on the revenues from their own land. This resulted in the categories small and marginal farmers, and agricultural labourers. All three studies also examined such categories as age, marital status and degree of social influence. The India study also pointed out two other important categories: beneficiaries and non-beneficiaries. In practice, however, it is difficult to predict who will benefit from a project intervention, even if the target group is clearly defined in the project documents. In Bolivia and Burkina Faso this differentiation was clearly impossible, as the beneficiaries of the project had not been defined.

Study techniques

Besides the rapid rural appraisal (RRA) techniques requested in the terms of reference, various other methods – such as individual interviews following group discussions – were used in the gender analyses to collect and check information.

Data on the division of labour and gender-related use of resources was systematically collected from men and women, both at household and community level. Information on the perceptions and self-image of women, their participation in decision-making and organizations, and their needs and expectations, was collected from women and men in mixed or separate sessions. This information was primarily used to analyse the position of women, in line with the specific requirements set for the pilot study.

The Bolivian study analysed both the men's perception of women and women's own self-image; the Indian study analysed women's self-image and their perception of men, and the Burkina study examined only women's self-image. The following aspects provided information on perceptions of women and their self-image:

- perception of women's role in relation to their husbands, co-wives, children, extension workers and strangers, and women's view of their role in village organizations;
- communication between women and others and the extent to which women take

initiatives within the family and communal organizations;
- degree of passive acceptance of their own situation;
- self-confidence in expressing themselves;
- men's perception of women.

The analysis of the gender division of labour and access to and control over resources was based on the Harvard Analytical Framework mentioned above. Although useful for describing the division of labour between men and women and access to resources, this did not allow sufficient insight into existing power relations in particular situations. Questions about women's participation in decision-making, and their control over resources and income as compared to men's, are difficult to ask because they directly address power relations between men and women. Moreover, both men and women – particularly landless labourers and members of marginal farm households who can barely survive as it is – often found such questions irrelevant.

The fact that, in Bolivia and Burkina Faso, villages had not yet been selected, also affected the analysis of the target group's expectations regarding the impact of project interventions. Villages for which project interventions have been planned allow a far more specific analysis than those uncertain of being included in the project: there questions and discussions must be handled carefully, to avoid raising false expectations. In Bolivia and Burkina Faso expectations could thus only be studied in terms of needs and/or experiences with earlier interventions. Therefore the assessment of 'impacts' of proposed interventions was somewhat hypothetical since they could not be compared with actual interventions. The India case study did manage to make such a comparison by analysing the effects on those who benefited from interventions and those who did not in two villages with existing irrigation schemes.

Rapid rural appraisal techniques
Rapid rural appraisal techniques (used, as noted, in compliance with the terms of reference of the contract for the case studies) have some constraints which must be mentioned. Although RRA techniques are meant to be participatory, the population or target group can only participate within the boundaries established by the researchers. This 'participation' in the research is only functional for the researchers: unless the population has some control over how the research results are applied, they are merely the object of research. Moreover, time-consuming 'participatory methods' cannot be squeezed into four days of fieldwork. Women often had no time for and apparently did not like such 'participatory methods'.

The disadvantage of RRA techniques – as developed in manuals to date – is that they do not encourage proper differentiation within the target group. This makes it difficult to give due weight to its heterogeneity, for instance, to social categories or households managed by women. The techniques are not always adequate to detect relevant nuances: careful design remains essential.

RRA techniques can become an end in themselves, as researchers using them get excited about the results as visualized by the villagers in paintings and drawings. It is easy to collect too much and too general data, which is difficult to analyse properly. RRA exercises in villages may well be suitable for doing baseline studies of gender division of labour or gender needs at household or community level. They do not, however, give sufficient insight into the power relations at household, village and societal levels, nor into the macro factors influencing them. Therefore a gender assessment study must combine RRA techniques with other complementary techniques such as secondary data reviews and in-depth interviews.

Lastly, the three case studies show that in using RRA techniques gender only becomes an explicit factor if the researchers have a conceptual understanding of it, plus the specific skills needed to deal with gender issues in a field study.

Institutional analysis

The analyses at macro and microlevels provide the setting within which the institutional analysis must be understood. The original methodology indicated two subjects for the institutional analysis:

- identification of perceptions and attitudes regarding gender issues among male and female staff of the institutions concerned;
- identification of institutional constraints and opportunities for implementing a gender oriented project.

All three case studies analysed perceptions – and to a lesser extent attitudes – regarding gender issues. In workshops with staff of the implementing institutions, topics discussed included the way activities were implemented, attitudes towards indigenous knowledge, ideas about women's participation, knowledge of institutional policy, and the need for field workers to improve their work for and with women.

Attention was also paid to the existence of a gender policy within the institutions and their capacities for implementation, planning and cooperation with other institutions, where relevant. In the case of Bolivia, for example, the organization that is to implement the project has a rather clear women and development policy, but this has not been operationalized in the project proposal. The institutions examined in India and Burkina Faso have no gender policy at all. In India, constraints and opportunities related to the development of a gender-sensitive approach were identified using means such as discussions on the strong and weak points of the organizations. The large number of institutions (primarily government departments) involved in implementing the Burkina Faso project made the institutional setting, and therefore the analysis of strengths and weaknesses, more complex.

It can be concluded that, in view of its importance for improving project planning, the institutional analysis received too little attention. The amount of time and attention devoted to the field work (the gender analysis for example) left too little time for the institutional aspect. A systematic examination of the skills, knowledge and attitudes of staff in the implementing institutions concerned would pay off in the long run.

Project analysis

Information about the macro and micro context, with a critical analysis of the institutional setting, provides the framework into which a project proposal should fit. The analysis of the project proposal is based on the project documents.[2] In the three case studies the formulation document (India and Burkina Faso) or appraisal document (Bolivia) was analysed, together with other documents of the institutions if available. The analysis of the document contents answered questions relating to:
- the way a gender differentiation had been made;
- the internal consistency of the proposed interventions from a gender perspective; that is, the degree of consistency among objectives, strategy, activities, inputs and expected outputs;
- the justification of the underlying assumptions and feasibility of proposed interventions from a gender perspective;
- the possibilities for the target group in general and women in particular to be involved in project decisions, and to participate effectively at each stage of the project.

The amount of information available in the project documents determines the depth of the project analysis, and the extent to which it can be related to the other components of a gender assessment study. When project interventions have been specified, as in India, they can be assessed in relation to the context, the institutional and the gender analyses. The Bolivia pilot study was able to assess the implementing agency's general women and development policy as well as the project's objectives and strategy. In Burkina Faso, however, only the project objectives and approach could be compared with the results of the gender analysis to assess their possible impact on gender relations.

Summary

The researchers worked within the methodological framework of the gender assessment study in three countries. Their experiences indicate that more time must be devoted to the institutional analysis, and that both the institutional and project analyses need further refinement. Further conclusions about the general methodology of a gender assessment study are presented in Chapter 5.

Notes

1. All three case studies used the same general selection criteria: access to town and/or markets, presence of services and contacts with external organizations. Other criteria were specific to the type of project or the socioeconomic situation (see the chapters concerned). Since the pilot studies were largely qualitative and participatory in approach, the number of research villages was limited to four in Bolivia and India, and six in Burkina Faso.

2. This means that the project documents must be taken as the researchers' starting point for the analysis, even though these cannot possibly reflect all of the ideas, discussions, attitudes and so forth of the organizations which are involved.

Bibliography

CEPAL (1982) Women and development. Guidelines for programme and project planning. United Nations, New York.

CIDA (1991) Two halves make a whole: balancing gender relations in development. Canadian Council for International Cooperation, Ottawa.

Coady International Institute (1989) A handbook for social/gender analysis. Prepared for CIDA. Ottawa.

DGIS (1990) A world of difference. A new framework for development cooperation in the 1990s. Policy document of the Directorate General for International Cooperation, Netherlands Ministry of Foreign Affairs. SDU Publishers, The Hague.

DGIS (1992) Women in development: advancing towards autonomy. The Hague.

Gianotten, V. and E. Barrón (1992) Análisis de género y estudio de impacto ex-ante de un proyecto de recursos naturales renovables de la Región Chuquisaca Centro (Gender analysis and ex-ante impact study of a renewable natural resources project in the Central Chuquisaca Region). Royal Tropical Institute (KIT), Amsterdam.

Gianotten, V. et al. (1992) Methodologisch verslag van drie effect-studies: armoede, vrouwen en ontwikkeling, milieu. (Methodological report of three impact studies: poverty, women and development, environment.) Royal Tropical Institute (KIT), Amsterdam.

Lingen, A. (1992) List of RRA/PRA tools. ISSAS, The Hague.

Lingen, A. (1994) Gender assessment study: a guide for policy staff. DGIS, The Hague.

Lycklama à Nijeholt, G. (1987) The fallacy of integration: the UN strategy of integrating women into development revisted. Netherlands Review of Development Studies, vol. 1, pp. 57–71.

Moser, C.O.N. (1993) Gender planning and development. Theory, practice and training. Routledge, London.

Overholt, C. et al. (1985) A case book. Gender roles in development projects. Kumarian Press, West Hartford, USA.

Walsum, E.M. van, et al. (1993a) Gender impact study in the Andhra Pradesh Surface Water Lift Irrigation Schemes and Groundwater Borewell Irrigation Schemes, a pilot study in India. ETC, Leusden.

Walsum, E.M. van, et al. (1993b) Gender impact study in the Andhra Pradesh Surface Water Lift Irrigation Schemes and Borewell Irrigation Schemes. Report on the Methodology. ETC, Leusden.

Zuidberg, L. and K. Tall (1993a) Methodologisch verslag van de gender impact studie, uitgevoerd in Burkina Faso. Ervaringen van een pilot onderzoek. (Methodological report of a gender impact study, carried out in Burkina Faso. Experiences from pilot research.) Royal Tropical Institute (KIT), Amsterdam.

Zuidberg, L. and K. Tall (1993b) La prédiction des effets du programme de développement integré dans les provinces du Sanguié et du Boulkiemdé (PDISAB) sur les rapports femmes-hommes. (Gender impact assessment of an integrated development programme in Sanguié and Boulkiemdé Provinces.) Royal Tropical Institute (KIT), Amsterdam.

If women are given the opportunity, they are ready to state their opinions on the socioeconomic situation

(Photo: Vera Gianotten)

2

Bolivia

Female peasants as economic actors

Vera Gianotten

The project that provided the context for the Bolivia case study is the *Central Chu-quisaca Renewable Natural Resources Management Project* (Proyecto para el Manejo de Recursos Naturales Renovables de la Región Chuquisaca Centro) proposed by CARE, a North American NGO with a Bolivian branch in Sucre (capital of the Department of Chuquisaca). The CARE project will be implemented in association with CORDECH, the Regional Development Corporation of the Bolivian government.[1]

The Bolivia case study concluded that while a sound general women and development policy is a necessary condition to ensure that women's position and gender relations are taken into account, it is not enough on its own; general policy must be supplemented with an analysis of women's role in the project area to prevent wrong assumptions about that role from becoming the starting point for project interventions. For that reason, a gender assessment study can play a vital role in the translation of women and development policy into specific project interventions aimed at improving the position of women.

Before examining the results of the study, it is necessary to give some information in the following section about the research approach and methodology applied in Bolivia. The second section deals with the specific characteristics of the Andean peasant economy and women's position in Bolivian rural society. An analysis of the project's main characteristics and the institutional context, in the third section, is followed by the results of the gender analysis. Based on this analysis, the chapter concludes with some hypotheses on the future impact of development interventions on women's position and gender relations.

Research approach and methodology[2]

The CARE project gives priority to the management of natural resources. Therefore this is the aspect emphasized in the study, which focused on agriculture and livestock, off-farm activities, natural resources, financial resources and labour. The reason for emphasizing productive aspects is that Bolivian peasant women are usually perceived as reproductive actors, ignoring the fact that their productive role is just as important as the men's. A typical example is the Regional Development Corporation survey, which collected a great deal of interesting statistical data: it maintains that 94.1 per cent of the area's female population is economically inactive (CORDECH-COTESU, 1989).

However, the researchers could find no evidence to support this claim. The gender assessment study looked at:

- the socioeconomic, cultural and political context, in particular the factors influencing gender relations;
- the project proposal;
- the institutional capacity of the implementing organization regarding gender issues;
- gender relations in the project area.

An analysis of these four interrelated components enabled an assessment to be made of the impact of the proposed project activities on women's position and gender relations.

In preparation for the target group analysis at village level, selection criteria[3] had to be formulated. The researchers and the implementing organizations chose the following villages for field study: Pucará (70 families), Qewiñas (37 families), Fuerte Rua (100 families) and Otorongo (48 families).

The villagers have a healthy distrust of external development organizations[4] which implement activities and set up local organizations without even consulting the peasant leaders, let alone the general population. To put a stop to this, the communal organizations have decided formal permission must be applied for beforehand. However, despite this distrust and the fact that possible follow-up activities could not be guaranteed, the people were highly cooperative.

It was already obvious during the fieldwork that there was not enough time to explore certain themes in depth. Andean peasant women are not a homogeneous category; they differ in age, economic situation, social influence and especially in the availability of labour to help them in their work. Not enough attention was paid to widows with young children, for example, and it was impossible to get a clear picture of the complex system of wage labour. In addition to time constraints, it was difficult to achieve sufficient differentiation. The group techniques on which most of the rapid rural appraisal techniques (used at the client's request) are based are less suitable than individual in-depth interviews for revealing economic and social differences between families.

Secondly, it was impossible to get a clear overall picture of informal relationship patterns. In Andean villages the complex patronage system of mutual rights and duties affects the family economy and the division of labour and activities. Moreover, Andean people living in the mountains have established an intensive bartering network with family members who have migrated to the lower-lying areas. Many Andean families also have plots of land in the lower-lying areas, where they grow tropical products.

Thirdly, it was impossible to give the villagers adequate feedback. It was not possible to plan a follow-up visit for detailed discussion of the provisional conclusions with the people. However, meetings were held at the end of each visit for general discussions about the issues in question.[5]

Many factors, usually of a cultural and ideological nature, determine the answers people give, because the women and development theme is coloured by many ideological assumptions and preconceived ideas. Since relatively short field trips are not conducive to discussing the intimate aspects of family life, such themes as physical violence and control over one's own body[6] were deliberately avoided. But this does not mean women are not confronted with such problems in their daily life: men do use physical violence against women, women are abandoned, etc.

Rural society in the Andes and the position of women

Peasant women, mineworkers' wives and housewives have always played a prominent role in the political struggle in Bolivia. It was the women, with their massive hunger strike in La Paz cathedral (1987), who forced the military regime to restore democracy. However, Bolivia is also the Latin American country with the highest discrepancy between men and women where health, access to education and equity before the law are concerned (UNDP, 1991, p. 20).

The Bolivian government has only very recently recognized the necessity for a special economic and social policy geared to women's needs. So far, any attention paid to women's position has been based on the traditional image of mother and wife, with food donations playing a crucial role. Up until 1981 Bolivia received 21,580 tons of food aid, which increased disproportionately in 1983 due to extreme drought, and has since risen to an average of 250,000 tons per year. Combining figures for commercial imports and donations shows that in 1975, 125 per cent of the total national food production was imported, rising to 368 per cent in 1988 (Prudencio, 1991). Apart from its macroeconomic consequences, this policy also affects women. Targeting mothers as the best channel for food distribution has emphasized one aspect of women's reproductive role: providers of the family food; it has devaluated their role as economic actors. In this way the food distribution system has had an enormous impact on rural development proposals, which perceive peasant women almost exclusively as housewives.[7] There are 6,000 mother's clubs in Bolivia, with an average of 50 members each. It looks as if some 300,000 women have been organized in this way to serve as a channel for food distribution.

Women's position in Andean rural society

In a country where 65 per cent of the population is of Indian descent (Quechua, Aymara and Guaraní), women's position cannot be analysed without taking such factors as 'ethnicity' and 'culture' into account. Adequate development strategies from a gender perspective cannot be formulated unless attention is paid to the relationships between the cultures of rural society: the original Andean culture and a western, urban-oriented culture.[8]

The anthropological theory of Andean complementarity and reciprocity between families, and between men and women within the family, postulates complete equity between the sexes. This complementarity is also said to be reflected in private and public life – the respective domains of women and men – and to be a logical consequence of Andean family structure. According to this theory, there are no unequal power relations or forms of exploitation in Andean peasant families because they perpetuate the culture of their Quechua or Aymara ancestors. Based on the analysis of mutual dependence between men and women, the principle of complementarity is presented as a normative ideal (for a critical analysis of this theory, see Harris, 1985).

Though complementarity does imply mutual dependence, it does not imply equity. When a mythical gender equity is attributed to Andean culture, such aspects as discrimination, physical violence and unequal power relations are relegated to the background. The complementarity is actually asymmetrical, and is based on a hierarchical system and the underestimation of all that is female. The mythologization of Andean culture, largely the work of intellectuals, does not clarify the position of peasant women; it is rather a pretext for ignoring the unequal power relations dominating the families and communities.

Bolivia also has a westernized, urban-oriented culture with unequal gender relations. The prevalent norms and values of this culture rub off on the rural community, mainly because development workers (agronomists, sociologists, extension workers, anthropologists, etc.) are continually passing on their westernized norms and values to peasant families. The existence of unequal power relations between men and women is generally denied within the cultural environment of professional development workers. Instead, the status quo between men and women is taken as the point of departure for interventions intended to benefit women, which stresses the importance of women's (reproductive) role as mother and housewife, and overlooks the economic role women play in the production process.

The Andean peasant economy

Peasant women make a vital contribution to family income. They perform agricultural and livestock activities, process food and trade in products, do housework and work as small traders or (temporarily) as housemaids. They do all this within the framework of the Andean peasant economy, which has specific cultural, economic and ecological characteristics. To get a picture of women's position in Andean peasant society, some background information on the peasant economy is helpful.[9]

Most peasant households have several plots of land at varying altitudes, which therefore have different ecologies; that way they can spread climatological risks, and put together a varied package of agricultural and livestock products. The production and productivity of the major Andean crops and livestock show a tendency towards stagnation due to water shortage, deforestation, erosion, and natural catastrophes. Nevertheless, Andean agriculture is an important factor in the Bolivian economy, contributing just over 20 per cent to the gross national product and providing work for almost half the labour force. Therefore, far from being isolated units engaged in subsistence farming, peasant households are fairly well integrated into the Bolivian market economy.

The main characteristic of the Andean peasant economy is that households are units of both production and consumption, which in turn belong to a much larger structure: the community. Since the launch of the 1953 agrarian reform programme, Bolivian peasant families with access to land have been organized communally in *sindicatos*. The highest authority is the Communal Assembly, which elects community leaders annually and decides on such communal projects as the construction of roads and schoolrooms, the maintenance of irrigation channels, etc. The communal organizations usually own the communal pastureland as well.

The agrarian reform programme decreed that all men over 18, all married men over 14, and widows with children under 14 could regard the land they worked as their own property. This laid the foundation for an ownership structure that recognizes only men and widows as legal owners. Yet many peasant families in the study area still have no titles to their property. The majority have hereditary rights to hold the land in usufruct.

Andean women have the primary responsibility for stock breeding; nevertheless, extension is generally directed towards men
(Photo: KIT Photobureau)

Officially the land remains the legal property of the original owners (the *patrones*). This must inevitably affect, for example, the readiness of peasant families to invest in long-term activities – there is no legal assurance that they will eventually benefit.

For women, who are dependent on their parents' good will when land is shared out, the problem of landownership or hereditary usufruct is even worse. Another obstacle is the unofficial but prevalent system of *sirvanacuy* (concubinage). Since they are not married, the women in concubinage cannot acquire ownership or usufruct (e.g. when the man dies).

All peasant families with plots of land belong to the communal organization. Since membership is based on ownership or usufruct, it is the male heads of household who belong to the Communal Assembly. Only widows have the same rights and duties. As a result, the structure related to landownership or usufruct has contributed to the social and political power of men.

Analysis of the project and institutional context

The project analysis gives insight into the coherence and feasibility of the project proposal, and looks at the way gender issues are addressed. The closely related institutional analysis gives a picture of the institutional setting in which the project takes place. As a part of the project and institutional analyses, various activities took place: a content analysis of relevant project documents such as the project proposal, the women and development policy of CARE, and secondary literature; interviews and workshops with management and staff of CARE; interviews with key persons and organizations operating in the project area.

The project's assumptions

The CARE project is an integrated environmental management project, with three important underlying assumptions about the socioeconomic position of peasant households:
- the main cause of poverty is the degradation of natural resources;
- reducing the number of livestock, especially sheep, will prevent the degradation of natural resources; and that
- peasants live within a subsistence economy.

Though it is not clear which analyses these assumptions are based on, they have largely determined the kind of activity implemented by the project. It will not, for example, focus on commercialization or market-oriented production because of the above unverified assumption about the subsistence nature of the peasant economy. It is these assumptions, and the activities deriving from them, which have been assessed for their impact on women's position and gender relations in the project area.

Analysis of the planned interventions

The project's ultimate goal is to improve the socioeconomic position of 2,000 families in 40 villages through the rational and sustainable management of natural resources. The main objectives are:
- to improve the use of natural resources;
- to bring about a sustainable increase in agricultural production;
- to encourage the population to effectively manage the productive infrastructure to be created by the project;
- to encourage women's participation in the decision-making process regarding the use of natural resources and agricultural production.

The project document proposes training and extension in planning, organization, agricultural production and sustainable management of natural resources. These activities will focus, for example, on crop rotation, mixed cropping, seed diversification, seed improvement and veterinary services. Also proposed are such agroforestry and sylvipastoral activities as communal tree and shrub nurseries for firewood, and hedge planting to protect pasture land. Women are to manage the tree nurseries and vegetable gardens; special women's groups will have to be formed for the purpose. The proposal mentions about 20 more activities such as microirrigation; creating terraces; building roads, silos and post-harvest storage facilities; the installation of multi-purpose water systems; and the construction of embankments and channels for water filtration.

Regarding the organizational structure, the document proposes setting up environmental committees responsible for implementing project activities. Once the committees have been approved by the communal organization, they will operate autonomously. Two members of the community (a man and a woman) will be trained to supervise the project at village level.

The project document thoroughly examines women's role in the production process, reporting that women have little decision-making power and poor access to extension. However, as we shall see below, in the choice of activities to be implemented, this accurate observation has had less influence than the project's various underlying assumptions regarding women's position. In the project document the following activities and conditions are proposed, related to women's position:

- training and extension activities will be tuned to women's productive, administrative and reproductive tasks;
- women will be encouraged to take greater responsibility and control;
- environmental committees will be obliged to have at least two women members;
- at least one animator at village level must be female; she will give priority to working with women's groups for income generating activities (in particular tree nurseries and vegetable gardens);
- the project will recruit enough female staff to improve communication with the target group.

The indicators for achievement of the project objective of increasing women's participation in the decision-making process regarding the management of natural resources are: 60 per cent of the environmental committees will have at least two women as members; a female animator will operate in at least 60 per cent of the communities; and 20 women's groups will actively implement the proposed project activities (tree nurseries and vegetable gardens).

Institutional capacity in the project area
In the project area, not one institution works with an explicit gender approach or strategy. Sucre, capital of the department of Chuquisaca, is the only place where an NGO works with and for women, and then only in the city's marginal neighbourhoods. This NGO does have some influence in the debate on gender issues. In rural areas, CARITAS and the government work with women's groups for food distribution. The Catholic Church runs boarding schools where girls are taught housekeeping. The government runs several agricultural and health care projects. Two NGOs operating in the project area organize agricultural and livestock activities. Both work only with men, partly by forming small producers' associations. CARE is already establishing medical posts and latrines in parts of the project area, as well as training women in health care and nutrition.

Institutional analysis of CARE
To implement the project, CARE will appoint a team leader (international CARE staff) and a Bolivian assistant team leader. In addition, five technical assistants will be contracted: three agricultural engineers, one expert in agroforestry and fruit growing and one civil engineer. The project will also contract eight social workers, who will be responsible for training and the implementation and monitoring of activities at community level. In each community CARE will work with two village animators (a male and a female member of the community), who will not be paid by the project. CORDECH will

make available one agricultural engineer, one forester and one civil engineer, as well as land surveyors and bricklayers to implement infrastructural activities.

CARE has had an institutional policy and a national plan of action for women and development since 1992. Its policy is to strengthen women's role in the economic, political and sociocultural life of the communities by actively involving them in project activities. Consequently, CARE also actively strives for the greater participation of women in the decision-making process and for recognition of their capacities. To realize this policy, CARE proposes the following strategies at its own organizational level and at community level:

- train women and married couples in management, planning, administration, leadership and decision-making, to achieve more efficient use of natural resources;
- promote women's participation in small-scale economic activities;
- stimulate and reinforce local or second-level women's organizations, to increase women's involvement in other communal organizations;
- sensitize CARE staff to the importance of women's roles within the family, the community and society.

The staff of CARE are aware of the problems facing women and are prepared to work for women's increased participation in the decision-making process, but do not agree on how to achieve this. There has been no really detailed analysis of women's specific position in the project area; however, various assumptions are made: women need to set up separate women's groups; women will benefit from small-scale productive projects such as tree nurseries and vegetable gardens; women must be trained in health care and nutrition, etc. The interviews and workshops with CARE staff also revealed a number of underlying assumptions about women's position, which largely determine how institutional policy on women's position is implemented:

- improving women's living standard will automatically improve their position within the family and the community;
- if women are involved in the proposed activities, they will automatically share in the benefits;
- including women in the proposed environmental committees will automatically increase women's negotiating power;
- the stimulation of separate women's groups will in itself be enough to increase women's influence on the decision-making process in the family and the community.

The following gender analysis supports the assertion that a good gender policy at institutional level is not enough on its own. For example, the planned interventions are based on many assumptions about the peasant economy in general and the role of women in particular: assumptions that do not pay enough attention to the role of specific gender relations.

Gender analysis: background

The analysis of gender relations was based on data collected in the field. Further references were literature on the Andean peasant economy and the publications on gender relations in the Andean community. The Harvard Analytical Framework (Overholt et al., 1985), used to set up an activity profile, is extremely useful for making an initial description of the division of labour, but is too limited for gaining insight into existing power relations in peasant households and communities. For that reason, specially compiled questionnaires were used as guidelines for the group and individual interviews.

Description of the communities

The study took place in four communities in the department of Chuquisaca: Pucará, Qewiñas, Fuerte Rua and Otorongo. The main language in Pucará, Fuerte Rua and Otorongo is Quechua (the men also speak Spanish); interpreters were used in these communities. In Qewiñas only Spanish is spoken, so researchers could communicate directly with the population.

The villages, with 40 to 100 families each, are situated from 2,000 to 3,000 metres above sea level. Access is by unpaved road, which can be impassable during the rainy season. There is no electricity, no health centres and only one village has drinking water for 34 families. In most villages one or two schoolteachers teach two to four elementary classes respectively. About three organizations (governmental and non-governmental) are responsible for various village development projects. The communal organization is the most powerful of the various formal and informal organizations in the communities: women's groups, drinking-water committees, small producers' associations, health committees, school parent's councils and environmental committees.

The plots of cultivated land vary in size from 0.2 to 5 hectares. In the study area agriculture is concentrated on the low-lying land at the foot of the mountains. Irrigation is rare and severe problems are caused by erosion on the mountain slopes. Some irrigated agriculture is to be found near the river. Potatoes, wheat and maize are the main crops and peanuts, onions, peppers and vegetables are grown on the irrigated fields. Peasants use hardly any artificial fertilizer and pesticides because of the expense, preferring the manure of small livestock and other organic matter from the surrounding area.

Livestock is extensive and consists of goats, sheep and cows. Also of importance are pigs, chickens, geese and donkeys. The animals graze on open fields on the mountain slopes or on high plateaus above 3,000 metres. The poor quality of the pastureland results in a high rate of disease and low productivity of meat and other by-products. The forested area is gradually being depleted by charcoal burning, overgrazing and exploitation for firewood. Besides agriculture, livestock and cottage industry, seasonal migration is an important source of income. Men in particular migrate to the tropical area of Bolivia (Santa Cruz) between June and September to work in the sugarcane harvest.

The four communities – Pucará, Qewiñas, Otorongo and Fuerte Rua – are not homogeneous. Pucará has hardly any seasonal migration, partial market orientation and some potential for agricultural development. Qewiñas has much better market integration; seasonal migration has become a structural element, and it has reasonable agricultural potential. Otorongo, on the other hand, has a great deal of unstructured seasonal migration with few possibilities for further agricultural development. Fuerte Rua produces very little for the market and bartering predominates.

Analysis of gender relations

The gender analysis and gender assessment study focused on six aspects: the division of labour; workload; access to and control over resources, services and benefits; decision-making power at family and village level; perception of peasant women and their self-image; and women's needs and perspectives.

Division of labour
Analysing the gender division of labour is a simple and effective way of gaining insight into the internal organization of peasant households. It also reveals significant local differences, which must be taken into account when development interventions are formulated.

Agriculture. With the exception of ploughing, women do all kinds of agricultural labour: sowing, planting, weeding, fertilizing, harvesting potatoes, winnowing wheat, etc. The daily burden of working for a good harvest is equally heavy for men and women. Both worry about rain, hail, drought, seed quality, the quality and amount of manure. For example, all the poor women said they would like more animals for the extra manure.

In Pucará, Otorongo, and Fuerte Rua the same division of agricultural labour was noted, but a different pattern was found in Qewiñas, where the men perform all agricultural tasks between sowing and harvesting, as well as the entire grain harvest and the selection of seed potatoes. Only after the seed stock has been selected do both men and women divide the rest of the crop between potatoes for sale and for home consumption. Qewiñas is in a process of stronger market orientation, leading to changes in the division of labour and responsibilities. Men are taking over productive tasks traditionally performed by women (agricultural tasks, seed selection, etc.). This process is being reinforced by development organizations that focus exclusively on men when it comes to commercial production.

Livestock. Women are responsible for the animals:[10] they look after them, shepherd them and treat them for disease. An important source of cash income, livestock is regarded as a 'nest egg'. Women are fully responsible for small livestock (pigs, chickens, geese), a very important commodity, and many said they could autonomously decide when to sell them.

Food processing. Both men and women are involved in processing food. Men take the wheat and maize to be milled, which involves travelling relatively long distances. If there is no mill, or if it is out of order, women grind the grain on a stone at home. This is heavy, painful and time-consuming work because enough has to be ground for the entire family, the pigs and the dogs. Women also prepare other products such as lard, cheese and *chicha* (the traditional maize liquor), but men bake the bread.

Cottage industry. Women are more important contributors to the family income through cottage industry than men. Wool and its by-products are the main domestic products. Women spin and dye the wool, and knit or weave it into sweaters, bags, blankets and ponchos. Many women also make woollen products for sale or to barter for maize, potatoes, and so forth.

Labour power. Most poor women perform agricultural labour for others. They are paid less than men, because they 'do lighter work', with the exception of sowing, for which they receive equal pay, perhaps because it is extremely precise work which the men supposedly cannot do. Women often work in return for manure, men work to be able to rent an ox. Often, poor women look after other people's cattle in return for manure or half the calves. Finally, there are the systems of *ayni* and *minka*, where family members, neighbours and *compadres* (godparents) help each other on the land in return for food and *chicha*.

Trade. The respective tasks and responsibilities of men and women with regard to trade differ according to the family situation and degree of market orientation. A good deal of bartering goes on. Women barter their domestic products without consulting their husbands. Agricultural products are sold on the market, to development organizations (for example to NGOs), or straight from the field. Only men sell products to organizations, but both men and women sell directly from the field, usually according to pre-arranged contracts. The researchers were unable to discover who arranges the contract and who fixes the price paid by the middleman. Cattle are sold either by men alone, or by both men and women, who usually fix the price together. Women sell the small livestock, fix the price, arrange the sale and keep the money.

The interviews and group discussions brought out certain views that did not match reality. In Qewiñas, for example, both men and women said women did not trade. The reason both gave was that women cannot read and write, and therefore get cheated. Three things contradict this assertion: some men in Qewiñas cannot read or write either; other communities with the same or a higher rate of illiteracy do not use this argument, and the women of Qewiñas do trade in small livestock, without even consulting their husbands.

Reproductive tasks. Women and their daughters are responsible for almost all reproductive tasks (from cleaning the home to looking after the sick). Two activities need further comment. In the project area men have to fetch the firewood. But since this is women's work in many other countries (and regions of the Andes), development organizations (including CARE) propose to set up tree and shrub nurseries run by women, assuming that women will benefit most from a more efficient method of collecting firewood. However, it is the men who are most affected by the problem.

They have to spend several hours a week and sometimes several hours a day fetching firewood. Secondly, in all families husbands assist their wives during childbirth. Traditional healers or midwives are only brought in for serious cases. Yet extension on pregnancy and childbirth is aimed exclusively at women.

Migration. In many other parts of the Andes, the men migrate twice during the agricultural cycle: after sowing (November–March) and after harvest (June–September), leaving the women in charge of all agricultural activities between sowing and harvest. In the research communities, however, seasonal migration occurs only during the quiet agricultural period between harvest and sowing (June–September). Although women then act as heads of household (with all the responsibility that brings), their work does not increase very much in the men's absence: during this part of the year, there are few agricultural activities, and they are responsible for livestock and housekeeping throughout the year. The real constraint on their decision-making possibilities is that men do not recognize women as heads of households, even when the men are absent.

Workload
Both men and women have an excessive workload. Descriptions of a typical working day reveal that it is not so much the amount of work as the accumulation and overlapping of many productive and reproductive tasks in a single day that prevent women from planning their daily work and completely limit their mobility.[11] Consequently they cannot take part in outside activities (such as training and extension) or fill communal functions such as president, secretary or treasurer of an organization (which also involves travelling to town to settle communal affairs). Their possibilities to acquire a cash income are also limited. It is therefore necessary to make a more accurate analysis of women's excessive work programme, taking into account the complexity of their many different daily tasks. In the meantime, 'women's workload' has become such a generalization in development organizations that it is even used to justify not working with women ('they are far too busy'). Oddly enough, this argument is never used when one wants to work with men, although their workload is excessive too.

Access to and control over resources and benefits
Natural resources. Landownership is a widespread problem: the title deeds to most families' property are not in order. If deeds do exist they are in the man's name, but even if there are none the man is regarded as the owner. Some families give land to the daughters; in others, daughters are not regarded as rightful heirs. However, even if a daughter is given land, ownership remains in the father's name until she gets married, and the husband decides to get it signed over, in which case ownership passes from father to husband. But even if the land she has inherited from her father has not been (or could not be) signed over, it is quite impossible for a woman to claim it.

> *Doña Vicente*, from Pucará: Because we, and my parents before us, were tenant farmers we had no land. Then after the *medición* (agrarian reform of 1953) my husband was given two hectares – the authorities said only men had a right to land. Now my husband is dead and I only have a daughter. His cousins made me sign a

paper saying I will leave the land to them when I die, even the orange orchard I planted with my own hands. My daughter refuses to protest, she says it's no use: men will always get the land.

Doña Nieves, from Qewiñas: I have inherited some land from my father, the title deeds are in his name. Other members of his family want to take it from me and I don't have the money to get the title put in my name.

Irrigation water is also controlled by men. Women are not members of the village committee controlling the irrigation systems, therefore they have no influence on water distribution. Furthermore, the committees formed by development organizations for the construction of drinking-water systems are all-male. Once these systems are in place, the same men sit on the committees for water distribution and maintenance.

A drinking-water committee in Otorongo: Female heads of household were not taken into account in the implementation of a drinking-water project. 'We single women cannot work with pickaxes on the high mountainsides. That's why we couldn't help with the project and now we have no drinking-water rights.'

Financial resources. There are various kinds of informal credit. Men, and occasionally women, set up rotating savings and credit organizations (Roscas). Only men have access to formal credit, which is granted by development organizations[12] and generally given in kind (seed, artificial fertilizer) in return for a share of the crop. Women are not involved in arranging such contracts, in fact contracts signed by both men and women do not exist. But if families have difficulty repaying a loan, they usually have to draw on their 'nest egg': the livestock; the women may have to sell off one of their pigs to pay back a loan they were not consulted about.

In summary, the fact that women have neither access to, nor control over either natural or financial resources – land, water and capital – is a basic problem which puts considerable constraints on their participation in the production process.

Social services. Educational opportunities are generally minimal. Many men and the majority of women are illiterate. Most women only speak Quechua. The community schools teach only the first two to four classes of primary education; children who want to finish primary school and go on to secondary education have to walk considerable distances to the regional or provincial capitals. Facilities are poor: badly constructed buildings, insufficient chairs and tables, old blackboards, hardly any chalk and no teaching materials. All those questioned said boys and girls had equal access to education. However, they also said girls have to leave school first if money or labourers are in short supply.

Informal adult education, such as study days, courses, training and extension are usually just for men, but women are expected to take part in family health care programmes. Though development organizations say women's workload is excessive, they take it for granted that women do have, or are willing to make time for health care extension programmes. All the women said they would really like greater access to informal education on aspects of agriculture and livestock. But because they cannot speak Spanish, are illiterate, and cannot leave their village because they have to look after their children, they found it hard to imagine the existence of courses adapted to their situation.

> When asked how such courses could be adapted to their situation, the women of Fuerte Rua came up with the following ideas: training should take place in the community; we'll bring our children with us; they can take notes while we learn our lessons; we can make use of *ayni*: we take turns – some work and look after the children while others go to lessons.

Access to health care is very poor. Most people prefer traditional healers (generally men); only in serious cases, or if they have money do they go to the medical post or to hospital. Boys have priority. Among the reasons both men and women gave for this were that boys are more useful because they help with the work; they can also help their mothers later on.

Benefits. All the persons interviewed (men as well as women) said women control the family cash. It was not quite clear who ultimately decides how it is spent, though many men and women said women had most control over expenditure. When it comes to things like buying an ox, both have a say; women usually decide on the smaller purchases, with or without their husband's consent. However, women are not taken into account by externally implemented projects when it comes to market-oriented activities or granting credit. Consequently, their control over income and expenditure is being eroded, which could mean they will eventually lose their role as family 'treasurer'.

Decision-making power within the family and the community
Within the family, women probably have greater authority than is commonly supposed. Women's decision-making power is equal to men's regarding agriculture, livestock, trade and cottage industry. Moreover, women traditionally have greater control over financial matters.

While there is a degree of complementarity where the gender division of labour is concerned (except for reproductive tasks), this does not imply equal relations. The often advanced thesis that women exercise a great deal of invisible power within the family, with men taking no decisions in public life without first consulting their wives, was not confirmed by this study. Many women are unaware of what is discussed in the general communal assemblies; they know nothing about the decisions men make in other organizations, such as irrigation or environmental committees, small producers' associations, etc. Further, women are not formally consulted about arranging credit.

> The Otorongo drinking-water committee has a problem with the payment of membership dues. Originally, membership money was to be put in a fund to start a communal shop. Then the (male) committee decided to spend some of the money on repairing the water system, and lend some to earn interest. The treasurer now says there is not enough money for the repairs. The water is polluted and unusable. In protest, the men have decided not to pay their dues.

The women of Otorongo were asked what they preferred: not to pay membership dues, or to pay, if the committee were reorganized. They preferred a reorganized committee. 'We are much better at this sort of thing. We would hold more meetings and tell people what happens to their membership money. We would take turns cleaning the system. But our husbands always say the meetings are for them.'

The communal organization, regarded by both men and women as the most important in the community, has the most influence in public life and the highest negotiating power in society. However, only male heads of household have speaking and voting rights, and it is compulsory for men to attend meetings. Women may also attend but, with the exception of widows, single women and women representing their absent husbands, they have no right to vote.

Most of the women's centres, which originated with the distribution of food to nursing mothers,[13] no longer receive food. However, women continue to meet once a week to make money, for example, by selling food at football matches to finance the building of their own premises. The women argued that they do not want to lose their organization. Though important to women, the centres have little power: no significant decisions about the life and welfare of community members are taken there. Thus women do not belong to the main decision-making organizations, such as the traditional communal organization and all those created by development organizations. In this way external development organizations have reinforced a gender division between local organizations. They have also reinforced the idea that women are only capable of domestic or economic activities of marginal importance, ignoring the fact that in everyday life women already perform activities of considerable economic importance.

Perception of peasant women and their self-image
The perception of peasant women and their self-image are influenced by the cultural norms and values expressed both in Andean rural society and the urban-oriented westernized society. Andean rural society is not a static, unchanging culture but a dynamic one in touch with outside norms and values (introduced mainly by external development workers), which it may or may not incorporate.[14] Both cultures have helped to create men's negative perception of women and women's own negative self-image.

The landownership system and division of labour within peasant households have enabled men to play an active part in the communal organization, with full authority and decision-making power, excluding women completely. This is characteristic of the patriarchal Andean culture, which gives women a subordinate role. However, the lack of recognition of peasant women also springs from the patriarchal norms and values imposed by 'modern' society on Andean rural society. As a result, most women said they feel inferior and oppressed because they are illiterate and do not speak Spanish. Men agreed, reinforcing this perception.

In Qewiñas – the Spanish-speaking community with the strongest market orientation – women repeatedly said inability to read Spanish was their biggest handicap. Meanwhile, they have come to take it for granted that they cannot trade because they get cheated and cannot do managerial tasks because they are illiterate. In other, Quechua-speaking, communities, women did not say 'they got cheated', nor did they say illiteracy prevented them from doing managerial tasks. In Fuerte Rua, the most traditional community, the women believed they could perfectly well perform managerial functions if only they were more mobile. Some examples of perception and self-image of women:

> *Woman*: 'Women's lives don't count. It's better not to be a woman; we're only there for the men's benefit.'

> *Woman*: 'You might as well take daughters away from school; what's the point of educating them.'

> *Man*: 'If women have good memories, they could be educated. But since men are better at remembering things they're the ones who should be trained, so they can pass on what they learn to their wives.'

> *Women*: 'We can't fill communal positions; women don't have good memories; we can't read or write; we are not good at speaking; the men get irritated and make fun of us when we speak in public.'

> *Men*: 'Women can't fill communal positions, they are cowardly, timid and shy.'

Women's needs

Beside the need to solve landownership problems, both men and women expressed needs connected with the production process: irrigation, improvement of crop quality, improvement of pastureland; healthier animals; more sheep for wool production and so forth. Apart from the areas of health care mentioned above and, recently, courses to set up vegetable gardens, women's training and education is minimal. When told of the possibility to organize courses taking their situation and problems into account (illiteracy, Quechua-speaking and low mobility), all women said they wanted to learn more about subjects related to the production process: agriculture, animal health, improvement and management of pastureland, etc. However, women's most obvious and most frequently mentioned need was to earn cash. Their priorities were agriculture, livestock and cottage industry, all potential income generating activities. A few examples:

> *Doña Julia* (37), from Pucará, would like to irrigate her vegetable garden and have more sheep if their health could be improved; she would like to sell more products and learn more about pest control and preventing disease in crops.

> Single parent *Nicolasa* (18), from Pucará, wants to grow peanuts for sale; she wants to know more about controlling disease and pests in her crops so she can grow more and sell them at the market.

> *Doña Regina* (35), from Qewiñas, has cattle but no land; she wants land so she can grow potatoes and wheat for sale.

Doña Dolores (37), from Qewiñas, would like more livestock for the manure, and wants to irrigate her vegetable garden. She wants to improve her crops and increase production for sale.

Gender assessment study

It is no simple matter to give a verdict on the possible impact of external interventions on women's position. The research period was too short for prognoses to be made. At most we can only say why we think certain interventions might have positive or negative effects on women's position and gender relations. Thus, the conclusions presented here must be regarded as hypothetical. Secondly, the functioning of peasant households and communal organizations must be seen in the socioeconomic context. Many external factors of a social, economic, political and cultural nature are outside the control of development projects. Landownership problems, women's legal problems, pricing policy, national environmental policy, migration processes, food aid policy, influence of the donor community, and so forth are all variables strongly affecting the possibilities of development interventions to achieve their objectives.

A number of interventions proposed by CARE in the project document are assessed below in the context of the institutional and gender analyses.

1. The project document correctly states that both women and men are responsible for the entire production process (agriculture, livestock, cottage industry, trade and wage labour). However, it ignores the fact that women are exclusively responsible for reproductive tasks. The gender division of labour must be carefully examined to gain a more accurate picture of women's excessive workload: what does it consist of and how is it manifested. If women are expected to participate in activities connected with agriculture, livestock and natural resources without the question of excessive reproductive tasks being solved, the intervention will just overload them even more. Thus there is also the risk that women will then withdraw from the very activities that interest them most, such as the improvement of crops, seed and land; animal health; and water management for irrigation purposes. Therefore interventions must be proposed to lighten women's reproductive tasks.

2. The proposal to decrease the number of livestock is based on general environmental considerations and ignores the fact that livestock is the main 'nest egg' of peasant households. Women are responsible for livestock, yet they are not consulted about the 'necessity' to decrease stock. In fact, they would all like more sheep to increase wool production. The consequences of such a proposal for the economy of peasant households generally or for women's position in particular are unclear. An assessment of the livestock problem based only on environmental considerations is far too limited. The proposal's economic impact on the household as well as its impact on women's position also need close examination.

3. The project proposal overlooks the fact that women have neither access to nor control over water and land. In the study area the landownership problem is highly complex, and unlikely to be changed by any development project. But on the other hand, there are cases where positive interventions have helped to increase women's access to and control over land (for example, legal aid). Despite its complexity, this problem will have to be tackled if the development intervention is to achieve its objective of sustainable management of natural resources.

4. The main natural resource in the Andes is water, which determines the possibilities for agriculture and livestock. While women do have access to water, they do not belong to the organizations controlling irrigation water, a fact that receives too little attention from CARE. So far there has been no proposal for ways of increasing women's participation in the management and distribution of irrigation water (by promoting women's membership within irrigation committees for example). An improvement in the management and control of natural resources will not be achieved by excluding the women whose very survival also depends on access to and control over water.

5. Women control the household economy and have the most control over expenditure. Yet there is nothing to suggest that this is being reinforced; on the contrary, the measures proposed appear to contribute unintentionally to a process of marginalization. The lack of credit facilities (in cash or kind) for women[15] supports this assertion. If the objective is to increase the income of peasant families by investing in the production process, why exclude those best able to assess the usefulness of such investments? It is the women who have the information needed for cost–benefit and risk assessments.

   The situation in Qewiñas is a case in point. This community has the highest degree of market orientation, and only men have access to credit. Contracts are drawn up without women being consulted. Women are equally responsible for agricultural and livestock production, and they have most control over income and expenditure. Nevertheless, they are dependent on decisions made by men who belong to the (all-male) small producers' associations, established by different development organizations to channel credit.

6. It is still not clear why the project proposal to stimulate production for home consumption was given priority over market production. The fact that women were particularly interested in increasing their cash income by selling agricultural, livestock and cottage industry products cannot be ignored, if the objective is to improve the welfare of peasant families. Although CARE cannot fully control market mechanisms, it must examine the possibilities to increase women's cash income through the sale of commercial products. Production for home consumption does not necessarily improve the food situation, just as market production does not necessarily worsen it.

7. The factor of gender plays a role in the dilemma of chosing between market production and production for home consumption. Improving welfare, especially the food situation, by increasing crops for home consumption does not necessarily lead to a more balanced diet for women. A case in point is the way meat is shared among family members: the

husband gets the biggest piece, then the children are served; women get the leftovers. If the project's encouragement of vegetable gardens is intended to improve women's diet, it must be realized that while this may help to improve their families' general health, there is no guarantee women themselves will benefit.

8. Women's organizations have had a positive impact in other regions and in other countries,[16] but this cannot be said of the study area. Mothers' clubs or women's centres have existed there for over 15 years, but continue to have little or no impact on public life, and in the present situation another 20 years could pass before they do. New ways of reinforcing their (highly limited) potential need to be developed.

9. Encouraged by development organizations, an incorrect view of the gender division of labour has been emphasized, in which men are responsible for the productive tasks and women for the reproductive tasks. This has lead to women's increasing exclusion from decisions that directly affect them (agricultural and livestock production, cottage industry and trade). Men belong to the Communal Assembly, small producers' associations (as if women were not producers), sit on committees for better quality seed and seed potatoes, artificial fertilizer, etc. Women, however, are still being encouraged to participate in activities of marginal economic importance.

 CARE stresses the importance for women of 'small-scale productive projects' such as vegetable gardens, tree and shrub nurseries, small livestock breeding, etc. This, however, puts a constraint on the recognition of women as economic actors. The proposed activities are derived from women's reproductive tasks and have marginal economic potential. Thus few financial resources are made available for them. Using (or misusing) the women organized in their clubs, getting them involved in all kinds of 'small-scale productive activities' – most of which are not economically viable, let alone sustainable – is likely to have a negative impact on the position of women within the family as well as in the community. No feasibility studies have been made by CARE (or other organizations) for any of the proposed income generating activities.

10. The case of tree and shrub nurseries deserves special attention. Firstly, the argument that women are responsible for collecting firewood does not justify the conclusion that they should be involved in setting up tree and shrub nurseries: while this is true in other countries, in the project area it is the men who collect firewood. Secondly, the shortage of firewood ought to be the concern of the whole family, not just women, because it is indispensable for the preparation of food which everyone eats. Thirdly, peasant families cannot be held solely responsible for the degradation of natural resources; the whole society is responsible. For example, charcoal burning in the project area leads to serious deforestation; but the entrepreneurs responsible for it do not live in the communities.

 The project document proposes to establish plant and tree nurseries managed by women. CARE guarantees they will buy plants and trees for reforestation purposes. If the women produce plants, their sales are assured. However, the nurseries have not been designed as a sustainable long-term activity: no feasibility studies or marketing plans have been made. CARE takes it for granted that once reforestation has been achieved and the project ends, the nurseries will probably also cease to exist (yet

Andean women are the traders; however, their requests for training are rarely met
(Photo: KIT Photobureau)

another example of a marginal economic activity for women).

The question is whether nurseries will really help to improve women's welfare and status in villages, or are they simply a convenient way of achieving reforestation. Reforestation will certainly benefit women (and men and the next generation), and women are likely to get better at organizing themselves. But there are probably more efficient and sustainable ways of achieving it and of increasing women's participation in the decision-making process. It would be better to mention these objectives separately in the proposal, and determine which activities are the most appropriate for each one.

11. The women in the project area have been excluded from all informal education to date (except for training and extension connected with family health). However, the project proposal could certainly help to increase women's access to these services, if educational and extension activities were given an adequate methodological content. CARE staff questioned during interviews and workshops could not point to any specific educational measures to increase women's participation. If no special package is developed for women, including appropriate teaching methods and techniques, there is a risk of women becoming even more overburdened and losing all interest in such activities. The gender analysis clearly shows that special programmes are needed for women: the fact that most women speak Quechua, for example, and are illiterate, will have to be taken into account; the women are not mobile, so courses will have to be held in the communities at times convenient to them.

12. CARE uses only quantitative indicators to assess women's participation in various activities and organizations. This brings the risk of leaving out qualitative assessment and limiting the evaluation of achieved objectives to formal aspects: there will be more women in the different organizations, but will they have any decision-making power? Neglecting qualitative assessment could even have a negative effect if women get discouraged and lose interest.[17]

13. Many women will have to take risks. One thing that holds them back is their husbands' posssible reactions. Jealousy and physical violence are not unknown in the project area. If CARE wishes to further women's participation in the decision-making process, it will also have to consider the possible negative consequences, and make proposals to prevent them. An important part of such a process will be to discuss and analyse gender relations with men, and encourage them to change their attitude towards women.

In general, the gender assessment study emphasized the importance of gaining insight into:
- the relation between productive and reproductive tasks and the role of men and women therein;
- the consequences of certain interventions (from a global environmental perspective, for example) on the position of women;
- differences between men and women regarding access to and control over resources, services and benefits;
- opportunities provided by various communal organizations such as the Communal Assembly, women's centres, and small producers' associations for women to influence the decision-making process within the community;
- the crucial economic role women play in the household and in the community.

In conclusion, it may be said that the CARE project, thanks to its sound institutional women and development policy, does have the potential to help improve women's position. However, the proposed activities are influenced by underlying assumptions which are not made explicit and do not always reflect the real situation. Such activities could have a negative impact on the position of women and gender relations. Therefore, this study shows that a gender assessment study, with its interrelated analyses, can help to identify and give priority to activities that really can contribute to the improvement of women's position and to more equal gender relations within a specific sociocultural and economic context.

Notes

1. We are grateful to the management and staff of CARE-Sucre, who enabled us to make this study. Their open-minded attitude allowed us to appraise the project proposal and assess the proposed activities for possible (positive and negative) effects on the position of women.

2. The gender assessment study was conducted by a Dutch and a Bolivian consultant, assisted by an interpreter (all were women). It took place in June and July, 1992. The study was also part of another,

more comprehensive one: a poverty alleviation study and an environmental impact study were conducted simultaneously by four male consultants.

3. The main criteria were: differing altitudes and therefore different ecologies; degree of market integration; degree of (temporary) migration; access to irrigation systems; presence of external organizations and degree of organization.

4. In this chapter 'development organization' refers to: government, non-governmental and ecclesiastical organizations, as well as bilateral and multilateral organizations.

5. These meetings were primarily about the farmers' justified demand for definite follow-up activities useful to them. Since it was unethical to raise their hopes, the researchers decided not to commit themselves. For a discussion on the ethical dilemmas accompanying this type of study, see Vera Gianotten et al., *Informe metodológico de tres estudios de impacto: pobreza, mujer y desarrollo, medio ambiente* (Methodological report on three impact studies: poverty, women and development, environment), Royal Tropical Institute (KIT), Amsterdam, 1992.

6. A study by Pilar Saravia (1985) shows that even after eight months fieldwork it was impossible to find out who in the family decides on the number of children. Such questions are seldom discussed with outsiders, whatever the cultural context (from a Bolivian peasant community to a middle-class London suburb).

7. It is legitimate to ask whether the real reason for reinforcing women's reproductive role as food donation distributors is to preserve a structural element of the Bolivian economy and the economies of donor countries.

8. For greater insight into the tensions between the Andean culture and the process of *mestizaje* (mixing of races) and westernization, see the studies and novels of José Mariá Arguedes, e.g. *Formación de una cultura indoamericana* (Formation of Indo-American culture), Siglo XXI, Mexico, 1975 and *Yawar Fiesta* (Blood Festival), Ed. Horizonte, Lima, 1983.

9. For a detailed analysis of the peasant economy see the extensive literature on the subject, including A. Figueroa *La economía campesina de la Sierra del Perú* (Peasant economy in the Peruvian Sierra), Universidad Católica, Lima, 1981; O. Plaza (ed) *Economía campesina* (Peasant economy), DESCO, Lima, 1979; Debate Agrario (Agrarian Debate), Nr. 13, January–May 1992, CEPES, Lima.

10. In a group discussion with the researchers for the environmental impact study, the women kept saying the dogs look after the cattle, and explained in detail how they are trained. An interesting development project would be to improve the dogs' training, to lighten the women's workload.

11. The women of Fuerte Rua would love to attend courses on livestock but say 'It's very hard for us to leave the community, we have to look after our children.' This has nothing to do with lack of time; they just cannot be away from home.

12. The Bolivian agricultural development bank has been closed since the 1985 structural adjustment programme. Agricultural credit is now only available through the development organizations, most of which are non-governmental.

13. These centres were first known as mothers' clubs, then as mothers' centres; now the very same externally imposed organizations are entitled women's centres.

14. A group of men led by a professional woman made a daily activity profile, which made it look as if their families lived in the city. They emphasized their wives' reproductive tasks, maintaining they did no agricultural labour and spent little or no time shepherding cattle or looking after livestock.

15. Although the CARE project we analysed makes no explicit proposals for credit programmes, other CARE projects in the same area do offer credit facilities. Credit is extended to the small producers' associations for men (and sometimes widows) set up by CARE in various villages. The fact that only men have access to and control over the various credit facilities is hardly ever questioned within CARE. Only one female staff member said she thought this was unfair.

16. This refers to the history of women's organizations in Peru and Chile. Though they began as welfare organizations which reinforced women's traditional caregiving role, they also gained political influence at national level (see Loreto Jansana *El Pan Nuestro. Las organizaciones populares para el consumo* (Our bread. Popular organizations for consumption), PET, Chile, 1989 and Nina Delpino '*Las organizaciones femeninas por la alimentación: un menú sazonado'* (Women's organizations for food: a spicy menu') in: Luis Pasara et al.: *La otra cara de la luna. Nuevos actores sociales en el Perú* (The far side of the moon. New social actors in Peru), CEDYS, Lima, 1991, pp. 29–72.

17. In an interview, Doña Margarita tells how CARE is encouraging her to organize a group of women to make a vegetable garden and plant a tree nursery. She is unsure of herself, and afraid she won't be able to complete the 'task' properly. She wants more supervision. If Doña Margarita is not supervised the final result will be negative: she will think she has failed and feel left in the lurch. This will not encourage other women to take risks.

Bibliography

Anderson, J. (1990) Sistemas de género e identidades de mujeres de culturas marcadas del Perú (Gender systems and identities of women in specified cultures of Peru). In: Revista Peruana de Ciencias Sociales, vol. 2, no. 1, pp. 77–117. FOMCIENCIAS, Lima.

Casós, V. (1990) La mujer campesina en la familia y en la comunidad (The female peasant in the family and in the community). Ed. Flora Tristán, Lima.

CIDA (1991) Two halves make a whole: balancing gender relations in development. Canadian Council for International Cooperation, Ottawa.

Commission of the European Communities (1991) The integration of women in development. Why, when and how to incorporate gender into Lomé IV projects and programmes. EEC, Brussels.

Coordinadora de la Mujer (1992) Propuestas de políticas sectoriales para la participación de la mujer en el desarrollo. (Proposals for sectoral policies for the participation of women in development). Ed. Coordinadora de la Mujer, La Paz.

DGIS (1990) Ook wij hebben recht op leven - Nosotras también tenemos derecho a la vida. (We also have the right to life.) Report of the mission 'Women and development' to Ecuador and Bolivia. The Hague.

Fernández Montenegro, B. (1993) Los proyectos de desarrollo rural con mujeres y la medición del impacto desde una perspectiva de género. (Rural development projects with women and impact assessment from a gender perspective). In: Portocarrero Suárez P. (comp.), Estrategias de desarrollo: intentando cambiar la vida (Development strategies: trying to change life), pp. 273–294. IDRC, Ed. Flora Tristán, Lima.

Galer, N., Guzmán V. and M.G. Vega, eds. (1985) Mujer y Desarrollo. Ed. Flora Tristán, Lima.

Gianotten, V. and E. Barrón (1992) Análisis de género y estudio de impacto ex-ante de un proyecto de recursos naturales renovables de la Región Chuquisaca Centro. (Gender analysis and ex-ante impact study of a renewable natural resources project in the Central Chuquisaca Region). Royal Tropical Institute (KIT), Amsterdam.

Gianotten, V. et al. (1992) Informe metodológico de tres estudios de impacto: pobreza, mujer y desarrollo, medio ambiente. (Methodological report of three impact studies: poverty, women and development, environment.) Royal Tropical Institute (KIT), Amsterdam.

Harris, O. (1985) Una visión andina del hombre y del mujer. (An Andean vision of the man and the woman.) In: Allpanchis, no. 25, year 15, vol. 21, pp. 17–41. Cusco.

Hollingworth, S. and C. Bognetteau (1991) Central Chuquisaca Renewable Natural Resources Management Project, CARE, La Paz.

Jelin, Elisabeth, ed. (1990) Women and social change in Latin America, UNRISD. Zed Books Ltd., London.

León, M. and Deere C.D. (1986) La mujer y la política agraria en América Latina. (Women and agrarian policy in Latin America.) Siglo 21, Mexico.

Musch, M. (1991) Vrouwenbeleid SNV Bolivia: terugblik en voorstellen. (SNV's policy for women in development: retrospective and proposals.) La Paz, SNV.

Niekerk, N. van (1991) La cooperación internacional y la persistencia de la pobreza en los Andes bolivianos. (International cooperation and the persistence of poverty in the Bolivian Andes.) UNITAS/MCTH, La Paz.

Overholt, C. et al. (1985) A case book: gender roles in development projects, Kumarian Press, West Hartford.

Prudencio, J. (1991) Políticas agrarias y seguridad alimentaria en Bolivia. (Agrarian policies and food security in Bolivia.) CEP-UNITAS, La Paz.

Saravia, P. (1985) Familia campesina andina y la reproducción biológica: un estudio de caso en los Andes centrales (The Andean peasant family and biological reproduction: a case-study in the Central Andes). In: Allpanchis, no. 25, year 15, vol. 21, pp. 65–80, Cusco.

UNDP (1991) Human development report, New York.

Webb, A.K. (1989) Women and rural poverty in Bolivia, World Bank, Washington.

World Bank (1989) Women in development. Issues for economic and sector analysis. Working Paper, Women in Development Division, Washington.

3

Burkina Faso

Integrated rural development: for whom and with whom?

Lida Zuidberg

The integrated development project *Programme de Développement Intégré dans les provinces du Sanguié et du Boulkiemdé* (PDISAB) was selected for this pilot study. Two consultants (one from the Netherlands, one from Burkina Faso), together with a team of six research assistants, conducted the study during the second half of 1992. The methodological framework established for all three pilot studies (see Chapter 1) was used, including a context analysis based on the literature; a content analysis of project documents; an institutional analysis of the partner organizations implementing the project; and an analysis of gender relations at village level, including sociopolitical aspects and expectations regarding the proposed project.

PDISAB had already been approved and had begun; however, while the project document had been written, it did not give all of the necessary details. Consequently, the study made recommendations for improving planning, implementation and monitoring from a gender perspective. The gender assessment study also came to two broader conclusions. When gender assessment covers a project for which implementation has begun but for which the project document has not been elaborated, the implementing institutions should take the opportunity to elaborate the project plan in dialogue with the target groups. (However, achieving such a dialogue, as well as the requisite cooperation among the implementing organizations, makes heavy demands on all concerned, including the project team.) Secondly, if the objective to 'pay specific attention to women's development' is to become more than an empty phrase, the way the project intends to do this must be clearly stated.

Proposed interventions: their intended impact on women

This section gives a brief description of PDISAB's objectives and institutional setting. The project's strategy and proposed interventions will then be presented and discussed from a gender perspective.

Objectives and institutional setting

PDISAB operates in two provinces of the western-central region of Burkina Faso. It is a continuation of a previous Dutch initiative established to support the regional agricultural service. PDISAB, which will operate for a period of four years (1991–1995, budget Dfl. 4 million), was designed under the auspices of Burkina Faso's department of planning and cooperation. It was established because of the need for better land management as well as concern about the lack of cooperation between governmental departments and other development organizations. Overall objectives are to raise agricultural production without damaging the environment, and solve the rural population's most urgent problems related to water, health care, education and illiteracy. The project's specific objectives – to be achieved not by direct intervention, but by supporting existing departments – are reflected in its four 'domains of intervention':

- the increase and improvement of plant and animal production;
- the reclamation, conservation and rational exploitation of land;
- the creation of favourable socioeconomic production conditions for farmers and support for their individual initiatives and organizations;
- support for the regional planning process and reinforcement of planning capacity at all levels.

Several governmental departments and one non-governmental organization (NGO) work together within PDISAB:

- the former *Direction Régionale de l'Organisation du Monde Rural*, DROMR (Regional Department for Community Development);
- *Direction Régionale de l'Eau*, DRE (Regional Water Department);
- *Centre Régional de Promotion Agro-Pastorale*, CRPA (Regional Centre for Agro-pastoral Promotion);
- *Direction Provinciale de la Santé et de l'Action Sociale*, DPSAS (the Provincial Departments of Health and Social Services);
- *Direction Régionale du Plan et de la Coopération*, DRPC (Regional Department of Planning and Cooperation);
- *Direction Provinciale de l'Enseignement de Base et de l'Alphabétisation de Masse*, DPEBAM (the Provincial Departments of Basic Education and Elimination of Illiteracy);
- *Direction Régoniale de l'Environnement et du Tourisme*, DRET (Regional Department of the Environment and Tourism);
- *Centre National de Promotion des Artisans Ruraux*, CNPAR (the NGO National Centre for the Promotion of Rural Artisans).

The Regional Department of Planning and Cooperation (DRPC) has the task of managing and coordinating the programme. There are five technical (expatriate) assistants: four DRPC staff (one chief technical assistant, one women and development specialist, one associate expert on land use, one administrator) and one agronomist attached to the Regional Centre for Agro-pastoral Promotion.

Placement

The intervention area comprises the villages where governmental departments involved in PDISAB are operating. The project document for the first preparatory or 'inception' phase[1] specifies that experimental activities will be initiated in 12 pilot villages where an interprovincial committee of six cooperating departments, or as the case may be projects, have initiated erosion control activities. PDISAB intends to station the female extension workers recruited on behalf of CRPA in the pilot villages. In addition, experimental activities will be carried out in a number of villages where the agricultural department (CRPA) is doing pre-extension tests with farmers. PDISAB may also finance activities in additional villages in both provinces at the request of the partner institutions involved in the project.

Attention to improving women's position is a part of PDISAB's third objective of creating favourable conditions intended to lead indirectly to 'increased production and income and the welfare of farmers' (formulation document: PDISAB, February 1991, pp. 24–25). Improving women's position entails 'giving women access to the entire range of productive activities and assisting them to create conditions for true emancipation and financial autonomy'. This objective is to be achieved by means of extension, research, credit facilities and training women's groups in financial management. To that end, PDISAB reinforces CRPA, namely through the recruitment of female field staff for its extension service and the support of its Office for the Promotion of Women's Interests (BPAF).

PDISAB's strategy: participation and cooperation

The project's strategy is to stimulate the population to participate and to improve cooperation among the organizations operating in the two provinces. PDISAB operates mainly through governmental departments and must therefore work through these departments to stimulate participation. Consequently, it could be said that PDISAB's main aim is to support the government's role in regional development.

The project documents state that NGOs must be involved in implementing the project, but they do not elaborate on the shape of this cooperation. Nor do they list the NGOs operating in the project area. CNPAR was the only NGO to participate in the consultation meetings of implementing organizations during the preparatory phase.

The project documents neither specify the villages selected nor give details about the population groups who are expected to benefit. The beneficiaries are everywhere designated as 'the' target groups, without differentiating either between men and women or among various ethnic groups. The project aims to pay special attention to women. However, the project documents do not describe women's productive role or differentiate it from the men's role, whether with respect to production, the use of natural resources, or production conditions and organizations. The same applies to the participation of beneficiaries in project activities. Though the formulation document states that farmers' experience is relevant to proposed interventions such as agricultural research or women's activities, it does not make clear how either women or farmers in general can participate in these interventions.

Much depends on the way activities are elaborated during the coming early years. At the time of the case study, the programming of interventions in the villages had not yet started. However, it can be inferred from the kind of women's activities planned that the project team thinks mainly in terms of special activities for women, rather than integrating attention to women into the programme as a whole. The preparatory studies, proposed planning activities, and the training and support of female staff taking place at the time, for example, support this assertion. Women are treated separately in these studies and plans.[2] The training of female staff and the institutional support which must serve to reinforce attention to women are extended only to units or members of organizations that work exclusively with women. This situation is more likely to result in a specific approach than an integrated one.

Planned interventions and their intended impact on women
This section describes and analyses the elaboration of the proposed activities in the four domains of intervention, from a gender perspective. In the process of analysis, the plans were found to be generally incomplete and inconsistent. The contents of planned interventions are not described in detail in the formulation document (1991–1995) nor annual workplans (1991–1993)[3] for the initial preparatory phase. Two examples serve to support this assertion. Firstly, the documents indicate (in the budget) which departments or offices of a particular department will implement activities, but they do not state who will be responsible for implementing, monitoring, coordinating or evaluating them. Nor do they state what shape such responsibility will take within PDISAB. Secondly, with the exception of certain departments (health care and education for example), no quantitative aims are given for the proposed activities which PDISAB will finance: objectives, expected results and indicators for monitoring and evaluation are barely mentioned.

The interventions proposed for 1993 are intended to benefit men and women in a variety of ways, as described below.

Animal and vegetable production. PDISAB's interventions in this field support CRPA's existing activities (implemented through the provincial agricultural and livestock departments), and finance some of its operational costs. PDISAB also supports l'Organisation du Monde Rural (OMR) and CRPA through the following activities:
- intensification of agriculture, via extension to 1,800 farmers (male and female) and training of extension workers;
- research, including the creation of ten demonstration farms;
- the monitoring and evaluation of agricultural production;
- the improvement of animal production, via extension to 40 farmers and training of extension workers.

The lack of further detail makes it difficult to judge whether these interventions will have any differential impact on male and female farmers.

Land management and erosion control. PDISAB's land management interventions focus on the 12 pilot villages, where they serve as a model and must be related to other project activities. Guided by the staff of six organizations collaborating for the purpose in the provinces,[4] these villages will be the first to make a land management plan for their territory. However, the project document does not state which farmers or village representatives will draw up the plans.

PDISAB's support for erosion control activities is a continuation of similar activities undertaken by another project in the area (United Nations Sahel Organisation). This support includes free transport of stones and provision of small tools for participating villages. The ongoing costs of implementing organizations (CRPA, DRET and Betah, a specially created NGO) are paid by the project.

At present PDISAB's main concern is to design a cohesive programme of measures for erosion control and land management. However, it is not yet clear how the populations' interests will be taken into account: therefore the project ideas on erosion control and land management give no indication of possible gender interests.

Production conditions and farmers' organizations. The proposed interventions are intended to promote certain 'socioeconomic conditions': health, education, drinking-water supply, villagers' participation in their own development, women's autonomy and reduction of their workload. Interventions in the field of health, education and drinking-water that relate to the financing of infrastructure and training are elaborated in more detail than the others.

Interventions planned for 1993, particularly those aimed at women, come under the objective of 'strengthening farmers' organizations'; they are proposed by OMR, BPAF and the social services sections of the provincial health departments. These interventions relate to grain mills, granaries, shea butter presses, food storage, midwives' equipment, training in health and hygiene, and education. However, there is considerable overlap, because they have been proposed by individual departments. PDISAB has therefore called for further mutual consultations on these interventions before it approves their financing. Furthermore, the project plans to provide credit and savings facilities to farmers, to be set up and managed by the new female extension workers. It is not clear whether all farmers (male and female) will benefit, or just female farmers.

The villages were not consulted before the interventions related to production conditions and farmers' organizations were proposed. Some proposals were taken from a list of investments already included in the regional five-year-plan. Also, we noted that the interventions intended to support 'women's autonomy' or 'reduction of their workload' primarily refer to women's reproductive tasks (nutrition, water, food processing, clothing and health care); there is very little support for their productive tasks (storage of agricultural and horticultural produce and credit for small traders).

Planning. PDISAB will prepare a Regional Plan of Action for women, based on a study of women's position in Boulkiemdé and Sanguié (1992), and on strategies of the implementing organizations. In 1992, PDISAB arranged a number of meetings with the partner organizations to formulate a common strategy to improve women's position. In 1993, a seminar 'of special interest to women up to village level' was planned to prepare the Regional Plan of Action for women.

Two comments can be made from a gender perspective. One is the fact that the proposed plan of action for women is not related to the other plans which the project intends to support (the Regional Development Plan and the Regional Scheme for Environmental Planning) would appear to indicate that women's development is regarded as unrelated to mainstream development.

The second comment refers to the way the project intends to 'reinforce' planning by striving, for example, for a common strategy to improve women's position. A series of meetings[5] was arranged to formulate women and development strategies for the collaborating organizations. The one we attended clearly indicated a number of difficulties in working together. Firstly, there was no continuity: the representatives attending are not always the same, so they have to start over each time. Secondly, not only was the improvement of women's position a new topic, it was also one of the first specific topics for joint discussion to be addressed by the project. Thirdly, the subject proved to be too much for some participants. The result was a laborious discussion among people who are not used to discussing things in the first place! An additional problem was that the project team itself had little idea of how to conduct such a meeting, and could offer no proposals for achieving consensus and clarity.

A lack of focus, strategy and detail

The project analysis gave rise to several observations, which can be summarized in two preliminary conclusions. Firstly, the project's objectives, strategies and planned interventions lack a focus on beneficiaries; it is not clear which target groups are to benefit from the project. Secondly, the strategy regarding the participation of the population and institutional collaboration on interventions is vague. Consequently, the avowed objective of paying special attention to the development of women has not been integrated into the rest of the project. Several things point to this lack of integration. In the preparatory studies and the formulation of development strategies, data and strategies related to women's position are not correlated with other information, or with overall strategies for regional development or environmental management. Interventions targeted at 'farmers' do not give special attention to different categories of farmers (male and female farmers, for example). Insofar as activities are targeted at women, they are limited to women's everyday reproductive activities. Again, this is more likely to result in a specific project than an integrated one: women's development is regarded as unrelated to mainstream development.

The content analysis of the project documents points to a lack of orientation, strategy and vision of implementation, from both a general and a gender perspective. As we shall see, this lack of information is a constraint on the proper assessment of the project's impact on gender relations in general, and the position of women in particular.

Institutional analysis

Implementing organizations and their domain of intervention

In designing the institutional analysis, three seminars were held (two with regional or provincial staff involved in implementing the project; one with members of the field staff whom the research team had met in the villages). The aims were to collect data on the organizations and their staff capacity; to discuss perceptions and attitudes regarding gender issues; and, finally, to observe the capacities of the organizations as well as the project team to incorporate gender issues into their approach.

During the seminars with the implementing organizations, participants were asked to describe the main problems of the population in the project area, and say who was most affected: men or women. In this process:
• all organizations mentioned problems regarding poverty, health and illiteracy;

- certain kinds of problems were mainly brought forward by the departments dealing with them: lack of means of production were mentioned by CRPA, OMR and DRET; depleted natural resources, by DRET and OMR; planning and organizational problems, by OMR and DRPC;
- the organizations could not indicate any population category with a specific problem. The exception was BPAF, which mentioned problems regarded as specific to women, such as lack of access to means of production, and heavy workload.

When 'clusters' of problems had been identified, the participants were asked which organizations worked in which problem areas. Several turned out to be operating in the same areas, their activities either complementing or duplicating each other, but without any form of cooperation. Though this might suggest that the organizations get in each other's way, this is not the case. We actually met very few field staff in the villages. The field staff members themselves say there is a rapid turnover of personnel, and complain that their workload is heavy due to the large number of villages in their intervention areas.

Staff capacity

Male and female institutional staff are unevenly distributed by level within PDISAB's implementing organizations. Few staff are found at village level (25 per cent) as compared to the *département* (district) level (31 per cent) and the central level of the organizations (44 per cent). The total number of field staff in 284 villages is 341: 201 school teachers (183 men, 18 women); and 140 extension and other technical agents in the field of health, agriculture and community development (113 men, 27 women). Extension work is therefore mostly a male affair.

Female staff are poorly represented at all institutional levels; 29 per cent of all staff are women, with just 13 per cent in the villages, 31 per cent at district level and 37 per cent at central level. Though women are better represented at institutional headquarters, they hold positions of relatively little responsibility. Some of them work at headquarters simply because their husbands are stationed there. At the level of technical assistance in PDISAB, two of five specialists (all expatriates) are women (one supporting aspects of women and development). The project's Interprovincial Committee (CIC), comprising the heads of the implementing organizations, is completely male.

Existing and new structures to improve women's position

DROMR has a women and development unit (*Cellule d'Animation Féminine*) and CRPA has its Office for the Promotion of Women's Interests. In addition, the social services departments of the Provincial Health Service have an extension unit promoting family interests; this unit has initiated activities for women related to health, hygiene, nutrition, and grain mills.

PDISAB provides additional expertise at implementation level. It has recruited ten female extension workers (to be increased to 30 eventually) to reinforce CRPA's agricultural extension service, plus two female provincial coordinators to reinforce BPAF. By way of experiment, the former will work part of the time as regular agricultural extension workers, and part of the time on project activities coordinated by other organizations and project staff. Of the first ten recruited since March 1992, two have worked on the shea butter project at Koudougou and three are livestock extension workers. PDISAB is training these women for their future role as polyvalent extension workers (*animatrices*) for women.

We have observed that not only do the new female extension workers lack experience – except for those who worked on the shea butter project – but also several of them do not seem to fit the development worker profile of being willing and able to stay in the villages. Moreover, the project proposes that the female extension workers should live in the villages where credit and savings facilities are to be established. This means that, besides providing female farmers with agricultural extension, they will have to manage credit and savings funds as well as supporting additional activities beneficial to women.

As noted, PDISAB also supports DROMR's women and development unit. In fact, OMR development workers are much more versatile than CRPA agricultural extension workers. The project documents do not show clearly why the CRPA structure was reinforced with additional staff, instead of the other department, which already had female development workers in the villages.

Institutional capacities for cooperation and participation
One of the seminars for implementing organizations included a role play for the purpose of assessing cooperation between the organizations and project staff. The role play was designed to reproduce the project's strategy of cooperation, participation and attention to women. Divided into working groups made up of organizations operating in the same domain, participants were asked to formulate a project activity in the context of regular annual planning. They played their own roles of representatives of organizations, (governmental or non-governmental), technical assistants or project coordinators. They had explicit instructions to take women's interests into account in the project proposal. The following observations are based on the way participants cooperated during this role play:
- project proposals were extremely general. The role of individual partner organizations was not specified, so it was not clear who was to do what;
- there was no division of tasks between management and field workers. It was unclear, for example, who was to implement, coordinate and monitor a proposed activity;
- the project management committee, represented by staff members of the regional department of planning (DRPC) and the technical assistance department, gave the activity proposed by their own department priority, without discussing it first;
- consultations between the project management committee and various organizations were bilateral: the project management committee had the last word. It did not consult the other partners or technical assistants, or take heed of any suggestions for improving the proposal;
- the working groups were asked to take the interests of target groups, women in particular, into account, so they began to formulate an activity targeted at women. However, this was unrealistic, as most project activities were proposed without indicating a particular group of beneficiaries;
- participants were asked to keep to a planning scheme and specify their objectives, beneficiaries, strategy, programmed activities, intended impact (quantified),

Role playing among implementing organizations – government representatives and the project team –
during a workshop: a simulated planning exercise
(Photo: Lida Zuidberg)

expected results for the target group, indicators for monitoring and evaluation, implementation and budgeting. With the exception of one NGO, they obviously found it very difficult to express their ideas in concrete terms.

The project management committee itself confirmed the observed difficulties with cooperation in a progress report. It stated that the ten organizations' participation in project planning leaves much to be desired: most of the plans and budgets are too general and are submitted for approval too late; the project management committee and the provincial committee of the implementing organizations are unable to structure the programme together; certain concepts in the project document, such as the population's participation and collaboration with institutions for integrated development, need to be clarified for the partner organizations. The inadequacy of capacities for cooperation were also evident in the organizations' expectations regarding the project. Besides desiring its financial and material support, they hope for greater cooperation among organizations and better coordination of joint activities.

In addition to the problems noted at the management level of the project, the field staff felt their capacity to work with the villagers was limited because their regions are so large. They also felt restricted in their possibilities to take the initiative. New initiatives and supervision are the responsibility of their superiors at district, or even provincial or regional level. In our opinion the difficulties at both levels stem in part from PDISAB's own working methods, which do not stimulate partners to cooperate and are top–down as well. That is, there is room for improvement in PDISAB's procedures and working methods.

Ambitious institutional setting
The institutional analysis yielded several observations which influenced the gender assessment of PDISAB. Firstly, the institutional setting is very much dominated by government organizations. The institutional setting is therefore largely determined by existing power structures and the hierarchical lines of communication within these structures, which project staff cannot influence very much. Yet the project also intends to work through NGOs. Secondly, the project is regarded as a financial donor rather than a source of technical assistance. The project management committee's own working methods appear to reinforce this perception. Thirdly, the large number of organizations involved in implementing the project, as well as their hierarchical organization, make for superficial planning. The result is poor cooperation and limited participation by the population and field staff in the design of interventions. Consequently, the discussions held in the framework of the gender assessment study hardly touched on the problems and needs of particular population categories (gender categories, for example). Both knowledge and awareness of these problems and needs are lacking, and gender attitudes remain diffuse.

Context: development sectors and project area

Few sources for the context analysis were available. It is therefore based mainly on background information from the project proposal, as well as additional data collected from research in the villages. Secondary data was obtained from institutions in the project area.

The project area comprises the provinces Sanguié and Boulkiemdé in the western-central region of Burkina Faso. According to the project document, the area offers a dynamic, working population; the possibility of agricultural development, for instance by integrating agriculture and livestock, and conserving natural resources; water that enables low-lying areas to be irrigated; and horticultural and small livestock activities.

With 96 per sq. km. in Boulkiemdé and 45 per sq. km. in Sanguié, the region is relatively densely populated (over 600,000 in 1991). There is a good deal of migration from the north to the south of Boulkiemdé, where the Mossi people predominate. Sanguié has relatively little internal migration, but there is seasonal migration of young men to the Ivory Coast. The Gourounsi tribe, with its two sub-groups, the Lellé in the north and the Nuni in the south, are in the majority here. The Gourounsi habitations are more concentrated than those of the Mossi. The less numerous Fulani are found in both provinces.

There are major cultural differences between the Gourounsi and the Mossi, e.g. with respect to marriage and the impact of Western religions. While both groups are polygamous, Gourounsi families can be very large, sometimes taking up whole neighbourhoods. The greater influence of Christianity on the Mossi is clearly visible, while the Gourounsi – the Nuni in particular – are predominantly animistic.

Natural resources

Infrastructure – roads, schools, health care – is above average compared with other rural areas of Burkina Faso. Data on the research villages indicate the soil degradation and lower water level that are visible everywhere. According to the villagers, trees have been felled to make way for agriculture. Fields were close by 40 years ago but now are often far away from the villages. Grazing grounds are more often fenced in than they used to be; fewer animals run loose in the villages. A number of shallows have dried up. In some places rice and cotton farming have disappeared, causing people to leave their villages. The building of dams enables land to be developed for irrigated vegetable growing; however, the dams that are being built are often of poor quality. Ecological changes are more visible in the north-east (of Boulkiemdé) than in the southwest (of Sanguié). Consequently Sanguié has more abundant natural resources than Boulkiemdé. The depletion of natural resources probably affects the farming system, but we do not know whether or how it affects male and female farmers respectively.

Agricultural production system

In Sanguié, the Gourounsi have a different production system from the Mossi (the largest ethnic group in Boulkiemdé). Mossi women are known to be strongly integrated into the agricultural production system (Nagy, Ohm and Sawadogo, 1989). Not only do the women work on all the main field crops (white and red sorghum, millet and maize), but their workload exceeds the men's in everything except land preparation. Married men and women also cultivate their own fields. The main difference between Mossi and Gourounsi production systems is that Mossi women fully participate in the family cereal cultivation. Gourounsi women help only with sowing and transporting the harvest. In both groups, decisions regarding land used for family fields and individual plots, resources and labour organization are made by the male head of the household, as is customary everywhere in the Sahel.

To sum up, available sources of information indicate that both women and men participate in agricultural production, which is a result of both family and individual effort. The roles of men and women in agricultural production differ according to their labour input and participation in decision-making.

Gender relations at household and village level

The gender analysis carried out in six research villages examined division of labour and workload; access to and control over resources and benefits; participation in decision-making; organizational capacity; self-image of women; and the needs and expectations of men and women. As a prelude to presenting the results of the gender analysis, this section describes how the case study took social differentiation between gender categories into account.

Identification of gender categories

To compare the two largest ethnic groups (Mossi and Gourounsi), the field study was done in three Mossi villages in Boulkiemdé and three Gourounsi villages in Sanguié.[6]

Smaller groups scattered over the two provinces, such as the Fulani, were not included. The research villages' geographical positions also represented differences in physical and sociocultural environment. Further, research in the villages took place at two levels: family farming systems and men's and women's village organizations.

The families analysed in each village comprised a host family (approached through village leaders) and two others selected by a simple system of wealth-ranking, to include both richer and poorer families. Varying degrees of wealth – indicated by size of family (and polygamy), prestige and possessions (grain storage, condition of house and property, agricultural equipment and means of transport) – are not enormous and certainly not emphasized by informants.

Within the family, there are also definite gender differences based on sex, age and position. According to the family hierarchy, a man owes respect and obedience to the head of the family, his father's brothers, and his own brothers in order of age. A woman must obey the head of the family, his first wife, her husband's older brothers, co-wives who preceded her, and older women. The bigger the family, the more complex the pattern of decision-making and authority expressed, for example, in the division of labour and personal interaction. Such variety was difficult to capture in our small sample, but it obviously affected contacts with outsiders such as our team. When looking for respondents within families or village organizations, one reaches the men and women who are available and have authority. It was difficult to gain access to the busiest household members (younger men and women, married or unmarried).

Every village has various kinds of organizations. For the gender analysis, however, two 'modern' village organizations *(groupements villageois,* one for men, one for women) were selected through the village authorities. The gender analysis at this communal level relates to participation in village organization and decision-making, as well as to the villagers' needs and expectations regarding the project.

Division of labour and workload
Productive activities. Some differences between the Mossi and Gourounsi have been mentioned, with respect to family size, polygamy and gender division of agricultural labour. More specifically, Mossi women do all kinds of agricultural work; Gourounsi women are less involved in the production of family crops and sometimes farm out work (in their own or family fields) to younger co-wives. In both groups, some of the work on the family fields may be done by hired male labourers, depending on demand and whether they can be fed. The meals of hired labourers are prepared by the women of the household that employs them.

Where livestock is concerned, no gender differences between ethnic groups have been observed. Men take care of the cattle, which are shepherded by the boys. In the dry season, the oxen are often looked after by the Fulani. Men also tend the small livestock, which may be fed by men, women or children. Both men and women do poultry and pig farming. We were told pig farming used to be men's work; now they leave it to the women 'because pig farming is difficult'.

Fruit and vegetable growing are traditional individual activities (some are performed by men, but most are performed by women) in areas where enough water is available

Married woman helps in making a diagram of her daily and seasonal workload. The diagram can then be compared with that of her husband
(Photo: Lida Zuidberg)

during the dry season. Where vegetable growing is a recent introduction, it is done by men. Vegetables were cultivated in all six villages, but not by every family.

It is women's work everywhere to pick products such as *néré*, shea nuts, tamarind flowers, leaves of the baobab tree, flowers and nuts of the kapok tree. Yet some men now carry out these activities for money, with their wives' help. Women also process agricultural and picked products: *dolo* (local beer), shea butter, and *soumbala*, made from fermented *néré*, for sauce. This work is generally done during the dry season.

The division of labour in trade and industry depends on the product. Women sell grain on behalf of men, who take it to market, but this has changed a bit since the introduction of sacks and carts. Women sell their own grain (in smaller quantities) only in retail trade. Livestock products and vegetables are sold when cash is needed by those involved with their production (for example, women sell pigs; men sell goats and sheep when food is scarce). Women sell homemade food on holidays, market days or at fixed outlets. Both men and women also trade in articles such as clothes and kitchen equipment; however, only male traders trek from village to village.

Reproductive activities. These consist mainly of daily household work connected with the preparation of food, child care and the home. This work is done exclusively by women and girls. The number and heaviness of tasks vary greatly from dry to rainy season. If transport is available, men sometimes help to fetch water and wood.

The building and repairing of huts, granaries and sheds is done in the dry season. Men do the building and women fetch the water, stamp the clay and do the plastering. If cement is used, however, the men do the plastering.

Communal activities. Men play the major public role at village social events: weddings, funerals, circumcisions, and rituals using masks. Women's role at weddings, funerals and sacrificial rituals is to help, for example, by fetching water. When entertaining visitors, Mossi women remain more in the background than Gourounsi women, who have more freedom in public. Village leaders, such as the village head and the president of village organizations, are men. The most respected members of the community are old men, whose task it is to give advice on educating the young.

Various organizations are found in all the villages. These organizations are of two types, and almost always segregated by sex: there are traditional associations for communal work and mutual assistance of farmers, and modern organizations (*groupement villageois*). The modern organizations were created at the instigation of the government to transmit extension messages and services to the village population.

This description shows a largely complementary gender division of tasks in productive, reproductive and communal activities. Peaks in the workload of women occur at different times from those of men, who are busiest in October (harvest), followed by April–May (preparatory work in the fields). Peak periods for women are May–July (picking, start of work on family and individual fields)[7] and October (harvest). April is difficult if water is scarce.

Access to and control over resources

Access to means of production and to communal facilities is primarily determined by their availability at family and village level. Access to water and land, if there is enough, seems to be no problem for men or women. Personal plots of land are allotted to women and young men by the family head, who can reclaim them at any time. The more well-to-do families have ploughs or can borrow them. Availability determines women's access to ploughs, which are used in the family fields first. In the poorer families both men and women use hoes. While both richer and poorer families have access to means of transport, richer women have better access than poorer women.

Men and women have equal access, in theory, to services such as extension, education and health services. If these are outside the village, as health centres often are, a woman accompanied by a man can visit them if they can afford to do so. All six villages receive agricultural extension; however, the women said they did not participate in it. The women told us they did not get any attention from extension workers. If women want to travel, for example to sell their merchandise or get medical treatment,

Women and men in Savilli village made separate gender-specific resource maps. Existing physical and social resources could then be compared to past conditions and future perspectives
(Photo: Margriet Reinders)

they need their husband's permission and also have to inform the first wife.

The overall picture emerging from the resource analysis of some richer and some poorer families indicates a homogeneous farmers' community.[8] We cannot pick out any striking differences between the Mossi and the Gourounsi. The access of men and women to the available resources is clearly determined by their productive, reproductive and social roles. Like the organization of labour, the use of resources is largely controlled by family heads.

Access to and control over income and expenditures

The main products are derived from agriculture, horticulture, livestock and home industry. Field products are transported and stored by men and women separately. After harvest, women use their products to feed the family. When they run out, husbands contribute from their grain supply. After that, the head of the household provides grain from the family granary, which is also used for food at funerals and festivals, as well as for weddings and conciliatory gifts. Since most of the women's grain is used for family meals, their supply is the first to run out, but some of it may be sold in an emergency. Other women's crops (peanuts, peas) are for both domestic consumption and sale.

Grain from the family granary is generally sold to cover expenses. Money from the sale of products from the family granary goes to the household head, who may spend some of it on his wives. Women keep the money from the sale of their own products, but sometimes use it to support their husbands. Vegetable products belong to those who grow them. Most of the products from livestock which is held in common go to the household head. Profit from animals (pigs, poultry) goes to whoever looks after them. Home industry products belong to those involved in their production.

Both men and women spend money on food, funerals, their daughters' wedding outfits and grinding grain (women buy grain for daily meals, men buy meals for labourers and strangers). Both contribute to communal costs such as repairing the village pump. Men spend money on agricultural equipment (ploughs), radios, means of transport and their clothes. Women say they have no money for those things. The household head pays for ordinary medicine, but women also contribute. Other basic household necessities paid for by women include soap, petroleum, kitchen equipment, clothes and kola nuts. The main difference between men and women regarding control over products and expenditure is that men control a much larger volume of products and amount of money than women.

Participation in decision-making

Power and responsibilities within the family are clearly defined according to tasks. Both men and women have a certain amount of freedom to organize their own work. However, they are always subject to the household head's authority over all family members living on the same premises, or working within the family farming system.

Both the household head and married men – as well as the head's first wife – have noticeably dominant positions. In the presence of strangers, male–female relations are respectful and reserved. The household head has more equal relations with his first wife than with other women. Women's relations with each other are more open, but there too one sees respect and reserve in the first wife's presence.

The possibility for women to participate in discussions on village affairs is strictly determined by their limited role in public life and the scope allowed them by men. In Gourounsi villages women's communal role is more visible, e.g. in ceremonies and the activities of their organization (*groupement*). For example, women from Valliou told the men not to meddle in the affairs of their *groupement* (the first to be set up in the village). In Mossi villages the opposite was more frequently observed: when the men of Savilli told the women to speak up, they simply repeated what the men had already said.

Organizational capacity

Villagers' capacities for organizing themselves may be observed in the way they conduct their meetings. Meetings also show how information is passed on by the chairman and his committee or by an extension worker when he/she is present. The study showed that women obviously have less organizational experience than the men. At the meetings we observed, women (the chairwoman included) usually arrived late. They had been less well-informed about the place or the topic of discussion and tended to enter into the discussion less often than men. Women attributed their late arrival to the busy harvest, distance and lack of information. Extension workers gave women less help with conducting meetings or organizing their activities. Yet lack of organizational capacity does not mean women do not undertake activities if they are important to them.

The very existence of a large variety of women's organizations shows they have a function. According to our observations, women's organizational capacity is undermined by circumstances deriving from their culturally determined lack of 'space' and lack of support from development workers.

Women's self-image

Women in both ethnic groups say they must obey husbands and first wives, and have no influence over their children. Nevertheless Gourounsi women's profile of themselves reflects self-confidence, even pride, in relation to men. They feel that men respect and need them. They are free to speak in public. Mossi women's self-image is dutiful and puts men first. We found it quite extraordinary that all women said they received no attention from either the agricultural extension workers or the female community development workers, whom they had first met several years earlier.

Development prospects and needs of men and women

The inhabitants of all six villages see development in terms of living and production conditions. The men of Savilli and Masséré also value cooperation and good relations. Development prospects are also reflected in the way villagers assess their living conditions and in whether and how they think these can be changed. Such changes are almost always expressed in terms of needs. Both men and women believe living conditions have always been, and will continue to be difficult due to a number of factors, including lack of water; difficulty of access to health care; heavy agricultural and domestic workload; lack of education; and isolation.

Lack of water was particularly emphasized by the women of Masséré, who said people had been leaving the village since 1984 because of this. Women expressed the same needs as men: both pressed for a solution to the water shortage, for the completion and expansion of the school and the improvement of health centres. These things appeared to have priority. Also mentioned was the need for agricultural equipment, improvement of livestock and horticultural activities, and measures to control erosion. Villagers feel the government should provide or improve such services, out of concern for people's welfare. We were struck by the fact that both men and women put so much emphasis on services. This might have been because these services are already in place, but do not function satisfactorily.

Expectations regarding the project

The population of Boulkiemdé and Sanguié participating in our study knew nothing about PDISAB, and it was not clear to what extent proposed activities applied to their villages. Therefore expectations regarding their participation in PDISAB were examined hypothetically: assessment of people's possibilities to participate in or benefit from a project was based on their experience with preceding interventions and their general expectations.

Ideally speaking, villagers can indicate what they expect from interventions (including their own role in them); in practice, however, they have no say in the planning of development interventions on their behalf. After making a request to the government for a school or a dispensary, for example, (and perhaps having to make their request again) they have to wait for an answer. Their possibilities to get information and choose how an activity is to be implemented are minimal. Villagers expect the most initiative to be taken by those whom they consider authorized to do so: government representatives. In this context 'villagers' are apparently men: women leave these matters to the men and find it very difficult to talk about their experiences and expectations.

Possible impact on women: major conclusions

PDISAB's possible gender impact was assessed in three ways:
- the activities and needs of the population were compared with the types of interventions proposed, to see whether they matched;
- the proposed interventions, including their intended impact on beneficiaries, were analysed in relation to the target groups;
- the possibilities and constraints of organizations implementing, coordinating and supervising the project were analysed regarding a gender orientation to the project.

Proposed interventions

The activities and needs of the population in both provinces were compared with PDISAB's four proposed domains of intervention. This comparison showed that the domains are defined so broadly that they generally match the activities in question – which, for the population, may or may not justify PDISAB's existence. Men and women in Boulkiemdé and Sanguié perform productive and reproductive activities in the same domains, but their tasks may be either similar or specific.

Further, we examined the degree to which the proposed interventions take women's role, whether similar to men's or specific to women, into account. Analysis of the PDISAB project documents shows the project has no strategy for taking women's position in production into account; we feel this will lead to their being overlooked in the implementation of any activity related to agricultural and livestock production. Programmes are addressed either to farmers in general (taking no account of the needs of either men or women) or – where aimed specifically at women – interventions mainly concern women's reproductive tasks and not their role in production. Consequently, there is a definite risk that women's productive tasks will be neglected, if not marginalized:
- there is no guarantee women will in fact benefit from livestock and agricultural research and extension activities, because the project documents do not specify how women are to be included and/or will be approached in research and extension activities;
- support for women is strictly confined to improving conditions that 'indirectly' contribute to production: women's housekeeping tasks, health care, food processing, and storage of and trade in agricultural products. While these activities are all specific to women, they represent only a small proportion of women's total activities;
- the preparatory activities already undertaken by the project (studies and planning) treat women separately; this will result in a programme that is much more specific

than integrated;

- the training of extension workers and the institutional support, which should guarantee women are taken into account, are limited to units working specifically with women.

The conclusion related to these observations is that if research and extension are not clearly targeted, they will have little impact on female producers. Planners, researchers and extension workers must be taught how to take the activities of both women and men into account in their methodology and approach. However, this cannot be achieved by simply recruiting female extension workers with the task of 'work with women'.

Impact of the institutional set-up

Many observations regarding issues of gender and women's position were made during the analysis of bottlenecks and opportunities related to implementation, coordination and supervision of the programme. At the level of field staff, we observed that there are too few female extension workers. Moreover, the tasks of the project's female extension workers are not clearly defined. To make matters worse, women's perception is that male extension workers are not interested in them.

At managerial level, we noticed that though partner organizations would like to cooperate, the staff responsible for implementing the project realize their capacities for planning and cooperation are limited. Moreover, gender attitudes are hardly ever discussed; project activities do not include training staff to implement a gender-specific approach, despite the presence of a women and development expert in the project team. The tasks and working relations of this expert are not specified. The project limits institutional support for the promotion of women's interests to structures which focus more on women's reproductive activities; this support does not include training staff to develop gender awareness or a gender approach for interventions.

The major constraints on the project's aim to pay 'special attention to women' are thus the lack of awareness within the organizations of the real situation of men and women; and the project team's lack of vision regarding an approach based on this real situation.

Possibilities to avoid a negative impact on women

Both the impact of the proposed interventions and the impact of the institutional set-up lead to the conclusion that, in its present form, the project is unlikely to have a positive impact on women (or men for that matter). The challenge for PDISAB is to start an integrated project involving both the governmental and non-governmental organizations in Sanguié and Boulkiemdé, *and* the population. Taking up this challenge will require a fundamental reorientation and an elaboration of the project's ideas. Moreover, to achieve women's participation, PDISAB will need to develop a specific strategy.

Proposed reorientation of the project

The project could be reorientated in several ways. PDISAB could formulate the relation between the four objectives regarding its domains of intervention more clearly; the programmes and their priorities would then be cohesive. The result would be a clear connection among objectives such as increase of production, rational use of natural resources and the improvement of production conditions. This reorientation would enable strategies for including male and female beneficiaries to be defined in such a way that women's organizations and productive activities could be given proper attention.

To maintain major objectives, more emphasis should be put on the project's points of departure: departmental cooperation and the participation of the (male and female) population. The project's role of financier must be subordinate to its role of provider of technical support to institutions and interventions, including strengthening women and development efforts. Both human and financial resources must be reallocated accordingly. That is, PDISAB needs to be more cautious when selecting activities or villages, because it takes more effort to elaborate a participatory and gender-relevant approach to target groups.

The elaboration of a gender-relevant approach requires increased gender sensitivity in all project activities, whether they concern the planning and implementation of interventions or institutional support. Therefore gender training of both decision-makers and field staff must be included in the project activities. Such training must be combined with clearer differentiation of the complementary roles of collaborating organizations, and more clearly defined tasks, which would enable field and managerial staff to take initiatives.

We believe that although it is a good idea to include a women and development specialist in the project team and to use financing to reinforce organizational structures that can help to improve women's position, this alone is not enough. Firstly, the women and development specialists working within these structures have no decision-making power; they need connections with the project committee and representation in the project management. Moreover, the specialist's mandate must be correlated with that of her counterpart. Secondly, their job descriptions must include the development and implementation of training in gender relations, both at the level of the population in the project area and that of the organizations involved in the project.

Concluding remarks

The Burkina Faso study is interesting in that it was not undertaken to see whether the project should be carried out or not, as would have been the case if it had not already been approved. The gender assessment of a project which has already started has a somewhat different dimension. In these cases in particular, it is even more important than usual to answer several questions beforehand, and to make a good case for deciding to undertake a gender assessment. Firstly, who has requested the study: the donor, the implementing organization or the project team? In other words, is there an agency that will be responsible for following up on recommendations? Secondly, what is the objective of a gender assessment study which is not undertaken to provide arguments for approval, reformulation or rejection? It is possible to formulate recommendations to (re)orientate project activities, but is it also possible to recommend changes in the institutional set-up?

This study also demonstrates that a project proposal is difficult to assess when project activities have not been worked out in detail. That is, if the project proposal does not indicate why, how, when, for whom and by whom activities will take place (creating the necessary consistency), it raises the question of how to shape a gender assessment. The results of the Burkina Faso study therefore emphasize the importance of this general consistency, but are sometimes unable to cover gender-related aspects due to lack of information.

The study in Burkina Faso was also problematical with respect to the macro context in which gender relations and changes in these relations are to be analysed. Information on contextual factors could not be gained from literature or consultants who were knowledgeable about the area under study. This suggests that the design and methodology of a gender assessment study should pay more attention to the macro context.

Notes

1. Studies are to be carried out during this initial phase to plan future interventions.

2. We refer to two studies: a) *Etude sur la situation des femmes dans les provinces du Boulkiemdé et Sanguié* (Study of women's position in the provinces of Boulkiemdé and Sanguié), Provisional document PDISAB/DRPC, Koudougou, September 1992; and b) *Etude socio-économique de dix villages-pilote du Boulkiemdé et du Sanguié* (Socioeconomic study of ten pilot villages in Boulkiemdé and Sanguié), Provisional document PDISAB/Bureau AI-Consult, Ouagadougou, October 1992. With respect to plans, a 1993 seminar was to set up a regional action plan for women. Furthermore, PDISAB intends to contribute to a scheme for regional environmental planning and a (medium-term) development plan for the area.

3. The first two annual workplans (1991 and 1992) cover a period in which formalities and recruitment of project staff still had to be arranged. The 1993 annual workplan is the first to elaborate interventions through the implementing departments.

4. These organizations consist of five governmental departments (DRET, CRPA, DRPC, DRE and OMR) and a project called *Action Micro-Barrage*. The village plans for land management will provide a basis for the creation of future departmental land-management committees.

5. We attended one of these meetings in May 1992.

6. The six research villages consisted of three Mossi villages in Boulkiemdé (Savilli, Masséré, Somé) and three Gourounsi villages in Sanguié (Valliou, Farba, Ladiana). Somé and Ladiana are two of the project's pilot villages. The other four villages were selected from a representative sample based on the following criteria: ethnic group, average size of village, available infrastructure, distance from the main road, and geographical location.

7. Work in individual fields is done before and after work in family fields.

8. It must be borne in mind that this homogeneous picture could be due to the RRA technique used, which did not enable us to differentiate access and control between different men or women within the family studied.

Bibliography

DGIS (1991) Mémorandum d'Approbation (BEMO) Programme de Développement Intégré dans les provinces du Sanguié et du Boulkiemdé (PDISAB, HV/00/016). Directorate General for International Cooperation, Ministry of Foreign Affairs, The Hague.

Nagy, J.G., Ohm H.W. and S. Sawadogo (1989) Burkina Faso. A case study of the Purdue University Farming Systems Project. In: Feldstein H.S. and S. Poats, eds., Working together, gender analysis in agriculture. Volume 1: Case Studies (pp. 74–106). Volume 2: Teaching Notes (pp. 61–124). Kumarian Press, West Hartford.

PDISAB (February 1991) Programme de développement intégré dans les provinces du Sanguié et du Boulkiemdé 1991–1994, document de base. (Project document.) Koudougou.

PDISAB (1991) Devis-programme 1991. Koudougou.

PDISAB (1992) Devis-programme 1992. Koudougou.

PDISAB (1992) Devis-programme 1993. Koudougou.

PDISAB (1992) Procès verbaux de la première et de la deuxième journée de réflexion sur la promotion féminine. Koudougou, 14 avril 1992 et 9 mai 1992.

PDISAB (1992) Premier rapport d'activités du PDISAB devis-programme 1992 (mars–août 1992). Koudougou.

PDISAB (1992) Procès verbaux de la réunion du Comité Interprovincial de Concertation (CIC) du 18 août 1992 et du 5 octobre 1992.

PDISAB/Bureau AI-Consult. (1992) Etude socio-économique du milieu de dix villages-pilote du Boulkiemdé et du Sanguié, document provisoire. (Draft.) Ouagadougouo. (October 1992).

PDISAB/DPRC (1992) Etude sur la situation des femmes dans les provinces du Boulkiemdé et du Sanguié, document provisoire. (Draft.) Koudougou. (September, 1992.)

Tall, K. (1992) Etude préliminaire de l'étude-pilote du PDISAB sur les rapports hommes-femmes. Ouagadougou.

Zuidberg, L. and K. Tall (1993) Methodologisch verslag van de gender impact study uitgevoerd in Burkina Faso; ervaringen van een pilot-onderzoek. (Les méthodes utilisées dans l'étude d'impact sur les rapports femmes-hommes; expériences de l'étude-pilote au Burkina Faso). KIT, Amsterdam.

Zuidberg, L. and K. Tall (1991) La prédiction des effets du Programme de Développement Intégré dans les provinces du Sanguié et du Boulkiemdé (PDISAB) sur les rapports femmes-hommes. Royal Tropical Institute (KIT), Amsterdam.

4

India

Women may lose or gain: expected impact of irrigation projects

Verona Groverman and Edith van Walsum

Two 'twin' projects in Andhra Pradesh were selected for this pilot gender assessment study: the Andhra Pradesh Surface Water Lift Irrigation Schemes (APLIFT) and the Andhra Pradesh Borewell Irrigation Schemes Projects (APWELL). The Netherlands' development policy with respect to India attaches great importance to the land and water sector. In the past, the Directorate General for International Cooperation of the Dutch Ministry of Foreign Affairs has supported large-scale irrigation projects with a technical focus. More recently, there has been a shift towards support of smaller irrigation projects focusing more on gender issues and the participation of water users. The gender assessment study is seen as an instrument for further refining this present policy focus.

The major findings and conclusions of the gender assessment study in India[1] are described in this chapter. Several potential benefits of such a study are evident here: not only can it provide additional essential information about the impact of planned project interventions; it can also contribute to improved project planning, taking the impact on women's position and gender relations into consideration; and can lead to proposals to anticipate negative effects and strengthen the gender focus of a project targeting male and female farmers.

Like the other case studies presented in this book, the India study comprised four interrelated analyses: a project analysis, an institutional analysis, a context analysis, and a gender analysis in villages. A gender assessment study takes place within the framework of a proposed or planned project; the chapter therefore starts with a brief description of the projects selected for study. Based on an analysis of the project documents, it presents a preliminary assessment of the planned project interventions from a gender perspective. The following section covers the institutional setting of the projects. It describes to what extent the proposed implementing organizations do or could take gender issues into consideration in the context of their institutional capacities.

The impact of proposed project interventions on women and gender relations cannot be properly assessed without careful examination of the specific Indian socioeconomic and political context. The local situation in the project area must be taken into account as well. India is well known, for instance, for its high degree of segregation in socioeconomic terms. The following description of the macro and microlevel context is based on the outcome of the context and gender analyses carried out in four villages.

To gain better understanding of the gender impact of project interventions, an assessment was made of the effects of existing irrigation interventions in two of the villages studied in the microlevel gender analysis. The section presents some major conclusions about the gender impact of the proposed interventions. The chapter ends with a proposal for a gender strategy for both projects, thereby illustrating how a gender assessment study can contribute to better project planning. The methodology is discussed further in Chapter 1 (also see note 2 in the Introduction, regarding the specific report on the methodology).

Planned interventions: a critical assessment

A detailed content analysis was made of the APLIFT and APWELL project documents, appraisal and mission reports. Various aspects were critically examined from a gender perspective: in general, the relevance, coherence and feasibility of these documents were covered; more specifically, the consistency of objectives, strategies, activities, inputs and expected output; the justification of underlying assumptions; and the way a gender differentiation was made was assessed. Major findings of the analysis are presented here.

The planned projects

The APLIFT and APWELL projects have been through a long preparatory phase. In 1987, a first (fact-finding) mission discussed the findings of a groundwater irrigation project proposal by the Government of Andhra Pradesh. Meanwhile, the Andhra Pradesh State Irrigation Development Cooperation (APSIDC) had prepared a proposal for a project on surface water lift irrigation schemes. After several other missions related to both project proposals, a formulation mission was fielded from November–December 1992. One of the formulation mission's tasks was to screen both project documents, with the purpose of casting the projects in the same mould. The projects thus have the same overall project objectives and strategy. The only difference is in the type of irrigation scheme: borewell versus river lift.

The projects, planned for a period of six years, aim to improve the living conditions of small and marginal farmers through sustainable and environmentally sound interventions. The idea is to do this in such a way that women can become equal partners of the male farmers in agricultural and other activities. The immediate objective is to increase the agricultural production of small and marginal farmers in the target area by providing them with irrigation facilities. Women are explicitly mentioned as a target group, and the projects are intended to focus on the weakest category: households run by women.

APLIFT is to construct a total of 107 lift irrigation schemes, bringing 24,500 ha. under irrigation. APWELL will provide 5,400 borewell schemes, bringing 16,200 ha. under irrigation. The total project cost is estimated at Dfl. 32.7 million for APLIFT, and Dfl. 40.8 million for APWELL. APLIFT and APWELL have a similar institutional set-up and may therefore be regarded as 'twin' projects. APSIDC will implement the technical component, while NGOs will be responsible for the social component. The projects cover seven districts each, three of them overlapping. Both projects will be funded by the same external agency: DGIS.

Four stages – initiation, preparation, construction, and initial operation – will be followed by a 12-month period of after-care, carried out by NGOs. Activities will include feasibility studies, the mobilization and organization of farmers, and construction. Farmers will be assisted to organize themselves and will receive training in irrigated agriculture and other socioeconomic aspects. Farmers' training will include technical, management and agricultural subjects; training for engineers will cover technical and social subjects, agricultural extension and loan facilities. Irrigation engineers will be trained in organizational and participatory aspects. A Programme Support Office, the base of the Technical Assistance team, will coordinate the activities of the NGOs and APSIDC. As discussed in the institutional analysis, the arrangements between these institutions, broadly outlined in the project document, need further elaboration.

According to the project documents, farmer participation and the privatization of scheme ownership are key features of both projects. Farmers will participate in the design and construction of the scheme. Farmers' organizations will be set up. However, the project design does not go into detail on how to reach small and marginal farmers. We believe that to ensure the involvement of the target group, a special strategy will have to be developed to deal with vested interests at village level. Village politics are involved from the earliest stages. To classify as small farmers, for example, medium scale farmers in both projects registered land in the names of wives and sons. From a gender perspective this point is crucial, because of the considerable number of poorer farm households managed by women. Within the existing village context of vested power interests, women's participation in village-level decision-making is at a very low level. It would therefore be naive to assume that women will be able to claim their right (stipulated in the project document) to access to irrigation, unless it is backed up by special supportive measures.

Privatization is another key feature of both projects: one year after being commissioned, the schemes will be handed over to the beneficiaries, who have to contribute 35 per cent of the construction costs. The conclusion, based on financial and economic analyses, is that an 'average' small or marginal farm household with few or no outstanding debts will, with access to bank loans, be able to pay its contribution. However, we expect it will be very difficult for households with debt problems to acquire and repay bank loans. The same applies to the households managed part or full time by women; these households constitute 30 per cent or more of the total target population, since many men are away from their village for considerable periods of time. Without access to information and credit facilities, female managers/heads of households will be unable to comply with the scheme's financial stipulations.

Intended impact on women and gender relations

According to the project documents, the projects are intended to have effects at two levels. At farm level an increase in family income is foreseen, particularly in the income

Making a diagram showing shifts in cropping patterns over the last decade, plus the gender division of labour for various crops

(Photo: Annet Lingen)

of women and households managed by women. At project area level, a projected increase in agricultural income is expected to contribute to an increase in national income. However, it cannot be taken for granted that increased income will automatically lead to the increased well-being of all family members. The use of this income and the decision-making process at household level are crucial. Besides, comparing income before and after irrigation (in terms of increased income) obscures a number of qualitative changes that have an important impact on family well-being. As the case study shows, cropping patterns do change. Such changes sometimes result in a complete reorganization of the household economy, from subsistence to market orientation. This can have many effects, such as changes in food habits (for better or worse), in women's workload and the gender division of labour, and in the quality and quantity of fodder available to women for their buffaloes. Last but not least, irrigation contributes to a decrease in seasonal migration and to an increase in fallow dry lands. Though these changes are at least as important in relation to the long-term project objective as an increased income, they are more difficult to express in financial terms.

The project documents do not deal with the impact of irrigation interventions on the village economy as a whole. Interventions may have a positive spin-off in terms of increased economic activity, increased availability of goods, etc. Moreover, there will be a change in economic and social relations within the community. Relations between landowners and labourers change, as well as relations between various categories of landowners. Relations between neighbouring communities change too, depending on the degree of benefit each one derives from the irrigation scheme. Within communities there are beneficiaries and non-beneficiaries. These changing relations may imply increased tensions between and within communities. Sometimes there may be increased exploitation of weaker sections of the community, where women are relatively strongly represented. Both households managed by women and households with high male migration are an important part of this category.

Conclusion: a lack of gender focus
Female farmers and in particular households managed by women are a major target group. However, the only reference to women's participation in the project design is a general statement that training will include gender sensitization. Apparently the assumption is that if small and marginal farmers participate, women will automatically participate as well. Other categories of women are not differentiated – an important issue, as the gender analysis in four villages shows. Moreover, no specific outputs and activities have been provided to ensure the equal participation of women. Nor have any specific inputs and budget allocations been made (apart from a three-month consultancy for a gender expert, and a brief reference to gender sensitization as a training subject for NGOs). Both projects explicitly state that female and male farmers should become equal partners in agricultural and other activities. Nevertheless, the observations made above lead to the conclusion that the project designs lack a gender focus.

Institutional analysis

This section focuses on the institutions involved in the implementation of the two projects. General policy documents and reports of various organizations and programmes related to women and development in Andhra Pradesh were analysed. Interviews, meetings and workshops were held with the staff of relevant institutions.

The analysis focused on women's participation at various levels and at various stages of the projects, as proposed in the project documents and as envisaged by institutional staff. Aspects examined included assumptions (often implicit) about gender relations and women's position; constraints and driving forces within the organizations regarding the development of a gender-sensitive approach; and the practical relevance and feasibility of the proposed project approach for village women.

Institutional capacity in Andhra Pradesh
The shift in the focus of women's programmes from welfare to development parallels the changes taking place in Andhra Pradesh at national level. The state is one of the few in India with a separate Department for Women and Child Development. The department has an elaborate organizational set-up for reaching women at village level. The second half of the 1970s saw the start of development programmes geared to the credit needs of self-employed women and small entrepreneurs, as well as the establishment of training centres for women. Recently, the provision of credit and marketing linkages for those who opt for self-employment has been receiving more attention. But

there is still a tendency to initiate programmes at random without proper groundwork. Moreover, women's land-based activities, in particular critical issues such as women's access to credit and agricultural extension, get relatively little attention.

Institutional capacity of implementing organizations

As mentioned earlier, APSIDC will implement the technical component of APLIFT, while APWELL and NGOs will take care of the social component. The project documents have identified two NGOs: the Institute of Resource Development and Service (IRDAS) and the People's Research Organization for Grass-roots Environmental Scientific Service (PROGRESS).

Established in 1974 as a state-owned corporation, APSIDC has district offices in 22 districts. The total number of employees (all male) was over 2,000 in 1989–1990. APSIDC's task is to exploit irrigation potential. The organization is primarily involved in groundwater exploitation through bore- and tubewells and river lift irrigation schemes (from design to operation and maintenance). The main categories of beneficiaries are small and marginal farmers, scheduled castes and scheduled tribes. Technically, APSIDC is a very competent and smoothly functioning organization. One constraint on the development of a gender-sensitive approach – logical and functional from the organization's viewpoint – is that APSIDC has a strictly sectoral focus. Women come under the social component of the project and their role is therefore not considered relevant to technical design and selection criteria. Moreover, APSIDC has no experience as yet of working with NGOs. Nevertheless, APSIDC staff do recognize and appreciate women's role in irrigated agriculture.

NGOs are to play a crucial role in the project: they are supposed to mobilize and organize farmers, and train the various partners involved in the project in a variety of subjects. NGOs are also responsible for agricultural extension. They have been given no specific task regarding the women's component of the project; it was probably assumed they would take that on as well. The staff of IRDAS and PROGRESS are motivated and experienced in the social dimensions of irrigation management. They have good relations with governmental institutions. One constraint could be the extent to which gender concerns are integrated into their general approach. Furthermore, it is difficult to judge whether and how they can play a coordinating/networking role vis-à-vis other NGOs, as envisaged in the project document.

It is difficult to say anything meaningful about NGOs which have not yet been identified. Overall, NGOs are known to be more flexible and more committed towards the disadvantaged than government institutions. But on the other hand, NGOs may have conceptual and institutional weaknesses connected with the role assigned them.

As indicated above, irrigation must be viewed from a wider perspective which includes its unintended side effects and the problems women face: these might be even more urgent than better access to irrigation. We feel it is crucial to coordinate activities with other organizations operating in the same area, to enhance the projects' positive impact and reduce any negative side effects. Institutional linkages that are particularly relevant from a gender perspective could be identified. Three programmes worth considering are also financed by the Dutch government: Mahila Samatha (women's education), ANTWA (training women in agriculture), and the Water Supply Programme (drinking water). The Programme Support Office (termed in the project documents OSNAIP, Office for the Support of the Netherlands Assisted Irrigation Projects) has a potentially important role to play in strengthening the gender focus. It could also, for example, liaise with the three programmes mentioned. But to be able to do this, the office needs gender expertise. There is no provision for such expertise in the project documents.

Conclusion: lack of vision

The institutional and project analyses clearly indicate a lack of gender focus. Further, the project documents do not clearly indicate how this is to be remedied – how the institutions concerned are to develop a gender-sensitive approach. There is no explicit reference to specific roles and tasks regarding this aspect or to the requisite expertise. Perhaps this is due to a lack of vision, or to insufficient capacity to analyse information on gender relations. The results of the context and gender analyses presented in the following sections provide data that could be crucial to the development of a gender strategy for both projects.

Context analysis: rural society in Andhra Pradesh

Major trends in agricultural production are presented here. The analysis is based on the literature, supplemented with data from the case studies in the four villages.

Modernization of agriculture and its impact on gender relations

Andhra Pradesh has a predominantly agrarian economy; 70 per cent of the population depends on agriculture. The intensification of land use has been going on for a long time. Population pressure on agricultural land is high and ever-increasing. Irrigation is widespread due to the long dry season and irregular rainfall patterns during the rainy season. Traditional irrigation in the form of cascading tank systems has been in use for many centuries; controlled irrigation started over 100 years ago. From 1989–1990 the net irrigated area in Andhra Pradesh was more than a third of the total area cultivated. The process of agricultural change has been gathering momentum since the 1960s. The result is known as 'the Green Revolution' or, more modestly, the 'modernization of agriculture'.

Irrigation creates more work. Medium and large landowners hire more low-caste, landless or near-landless labourers. The majority of these labourers are women, as most of the work traditionally done by men has been mechanized. An important feature of the modernization of agriculture is the steadily growing participation of female wage labourers in the agricultural work force (in 1971: 52 per cent; in 1981: 61 per cent of the total female population in the rural areas – World Bank, 1991). The disparity between the wages of men and women is virtually constant (female/male ratio around 73 per cent; see figures for 1970 and 1985, World Bank, 1991).

The introduction of irrigation technology affects both women's workload and their role in agriculture. Women from medium and large landholdings tend to refrain from manual labour in the fields, which is regarded as a low-status activity. An intensification of women's workload can be observed in small farming families, who rely on family labour to cultivate their fields. When small or marginal farm families get access to irrigation, the women who were formerly involved in wage labour may then take up unpaid family labour instead (Royal Netherlands Embassy, 1990).

Major effects from a gender perspective
The modernization of agriculture has helped to bring about substantial improvements in the lives of small farmers. Food production levels and cash income have increased, tedious work has been mechanized, and yet additional employment has been created too. The provision of irrigation has drastically reduced the risks inherent in rainfed agriculture.

This process has also had a number of negative effects. Within the communities there is now a sharper differentiation between those with access to facilities needed for modern agriculture and those without it. Small farmers with access to irrigation and other facilities have become commercial farmers. Those without access, however, have become so marginalized that they have had to leave their own land fallow and labour on the irrigated land of others. Farmers and agricultural labourers have become dependent on market forces. The consequences include greater dependence on moneylenders and more debt traps. Moreover, a widening gap between men's and women's roles in the agricultural production system can be observed. Women still have no access to the less labour-intensive means of production or agricultural implements and tools available to men. Wage employment confers privilege in that it may improve a woman's bargaining position within her family and give her more control over the money she brings in. Below a certain level of affluence, however, this control only brings responsibility (World Bank, 1991; Sharma, 1980). Women's earnings are spent on immediate family consumption, whereas men use only part of their earnings for this purpose, keeping substantial amounts back for personal use (Mies et al., 1984; World Bank, 1991).

The increased use of pesticides has led to health problems. Female agricultural labourers who work daily in fields treated with these chemicals are particularly vulnerable. The transition from a traditional mixed cropping pattern to a pattern that emphasizes monocropping of cash crops, and the shift from payment of wages in kind to payment in cash, have aggravated food security problems, especially in households primarily dependent on agricultural labour. The major results of the gender analyses in the four villages presented below expand on this general situation.

Gender analysis

The microlevel analysis of gender relations and the target group's expectations of the project interventions took place in four villages. The aim was to gain a more detailed understanding of the implications at microlevel of the general trends outlined above and, against this background, to assess the likely impact on gender relations of the two irrigation projects.

Two case studies were carried out in Mahabubnagar District and two in Prakasam

District. These districts were selected by DGIS because both projects will work there, and because they had already been selected for an environmental impact study of APWELL and APLIFT. Selection of the villages was based on the principle of comparing and contrasting, using the following criteria: (1) three villages with lift irrigation schemes (two planned and one operational) and one village with an existing borewell scheme; (2) varying intensities of contact with outside institutions; (3) varying degrees of experience with irrigation before the scheme started; (4) varying access to markets and towns; (5) variations in cropping patterns.

Profile of the villages
Prakasam district is situated in the coastal region, the most fertile and therefore the most developed and prosperous part of Andhra Pradesh. It has a long history in commercialized agriculture: cotton and tobacco are important cash crops. In Prakasam 28 per cent of the total area cultivated is under irrigation, about half of it irrigated by canals. Food crops constitute 70 per cent of the cultivated area.

Mahabubnagar district is part of the Telangana Region, which is the most backward part of the state economically. It has a feudal history. Although the monopoly of big landlords, moneylenders and *jagirdars* (absentee large landowners) has been abolished, this feudal system is still reflected in today's social relations. Food crops constitute about 75 per cent of the cropped area. The area under irrigation is 15.6 per cent of the total area cultivated. The bulk of irrigation in this district is by wells and tanks.

Table 1 gives a broad overview of the four villages, according to the selection criteria used.

Table 1   Characteristics of case study villages

Mahabubnagar district	Prakasam district
Burgula	Garlapadu
· existing and planned borewells	· planned lift irrigation scheme
· about 5,000 inhabitants	· about 1,000 inhabitants
· contacts with APSIDC, NGO and other institutions	· limited contacts
· long tradition of well and tank irrigation	· tank irrigation
· easy access to markets/towns	· poor access to markets/towns
· emphasis on food crops and vegetables	· strong emphasis on tobacco, cotton and tree plantations
Chityal	Marrikuntapalli
· existing lift irrigation scheme (LIS)	· planned lift irrigation scheme
· about 2,000 inhabitants	· about 2,000 inhabitants
· limited contacts with institutions	· limited contacts
· tradition of tank irrigation, recent experience with LIS	· tank irrigation
· poor access to markets/towns	· reasonable access
· traditional rainfed crops + groundnut, paddy rice	· traditional rainfed crops (sorghum, millet, pulses)

The farming systems of all four villages have changed drastically over the past decades. There has been a shift from a strongly subsistence oriented economy towards integration in the market economy. Major contributory factors are:

- increased access to irrigation (this applies to Burgula and Chityal, not yet to Marri-kuntapalli and Garlapadu), the use of high yield varieties, fertilizers and pesticides;
- the transition from traditional rainfed food crops to (rainfed or irrigated) cash crops;
- increasing drought, leading to an increased tendency to leave dry land fallow and concentrate on irrigated agriculture and migration to find work.

All four villages have traditional sources of irrigation: tanks and *kuntas* (ponds or ditches dependent on rainwater). However, increasing drought and the collapse of traditional maintenance systems have brought them into disfavour. There is a keen interest in river lift irrigation or borewells. The villages studied have gained varying degrees of access to these modern sources of irrigation.

There are few formal and informal village organizations, such as mixed *sanghams* (village level organizations) and credit societies. The organizational initiatives that are taken by women in all the villages are of a very informal nature (see below).

Burgula is the only village where an NGO is active. The NGO informs men and women about government schemes such as the Development of Women and Children in Remote Areas Programme (DWCRA), which provides loans for starting income generating activities. The same NGO has also helped villagers to set up *sanghams*.

Gender relations
Identification of categories. An initial and crucial step in the analysis of gender relations is to identify various categories of women. The categories differentiated here are found in all the villages studied. The caste and class structure varies from village to village. Migration patterns also differ and, accordingly, the prevalence of households managed temporarily or permanently by women.

Women in lower class and lower caste categories are heavily involved in agricultural production, both on their own land and as labourers. The relatively high degree of seasonal male migration in these households means the women are de facto heads of household for part of the year. Women in landowning households which use both their own and hired labour do the same work as the women labourers, and/or supervise the labourers. There is no need for migration in these households because they can live off their land.

Another important differentiation among women is the extent to which they benefit from irrigation facilities. The majority of women in the villages concerned belonged to the category of households which owned some, mainly dry, land. In some cases they cultivated this land; in other cases they left it fallow, particularly when men had migrated. These women derived most of their income from agricultural labour on other people's irrigated farms. Very few of them owned irrigated land themselves.

It is also important to distinguish between age groups. Young women are actively involved in farm work and reproductive activities. Elder women are less active in the field, but they do a lot of work around the house. Adolescent girls help their mothers with many activities, especially in poorer families. If their mother's farm work

Girls have more work to do at home when their mothers go to work as irrigation labourers; this has negative consequences for their education

(Photo: Edith van Walsum)

increases, they take over work at home. They also help them in wage labour. But the more girls have to do, the less chance they have of going to school.

Finally, there is the distinction between married women and single women who are either divorced or widowed. Each village has a considerable number of single women: roughly 10 to 20 per cent of all adult women. Married women enjoy a higher status than those who are alone; they can share some of their work with their husbands, and economically they are better protected than single women. On the other hand, despite all their problems, single women somehow have more freedom and are less oppressed by their families.

Gender division of labour and women's workload. The following step is to describe the division of labour in agriculture, livestock production, and the reproductive sphere. The amount and intensity of the work and the gender division of labour depends on the agricultural season, the cropping pattern, whether the land is irrigated, the availability of water and other resources such as firewood and fodder, as well as such factors as class and age. Moreover, the type of work done by men and women who are only partially able to live off their own land depends on the employment opportunities in the area and the specific background of the household concerned. In practice, each village caste has evolved its own specific pattern of migration.

Agricultural production. For almost all crops men perform the operations using a certain amount of machinery and draught animals: preparing the fields, digging canals etc. Once the land has been prepared, women do most of the work. Men used to spray all pesticides, but now women do this too. Men put the finishing touches to the harvest operations (tying the bundles and stitching the bags filled by the women, for example) and take the produce to the market for sale.

Irrigation-related activities are shared by men and women. Men make the field bunds and usually distribute the water; women are involved in rearranging and maintaining field bunds, and so forth. When men are away, women take over their irrigation activities, or they hire male labourers to do this.

As noted, the type of work carried out by small and marginal farm women and female agricultural labourers is almost the same. The working hours of female labourers vary from village to village and season to season. Women working on their own land some-times have to supervise labourers. Women regard working in the fields as much more difficult than working at home. A comparison of women's and men's work in different crops shows that:

- women perform more agricultural operations then men. This implies that they are not only occupied with work for more hours during the day, but also that much is required of them in terms of managing their time and work. There are peak periods during the day and during the year, when they face serious stress because of the many activities they have to combine within a fixed period of time.
- men work intensively for short periods, whereas women have to work throughout the season.

Villagers differentiate between 'women's crops' and 'men's crops'. 'Women's crops' are traditional rainfed food crops primarily intended for home consumption; 'men's crops' are cash crops, which are usually irrigated. In both cases women do most of the work; the terms 'men's' and 'women's' seem to refer to the major destination of the crops, not to the amount of female or male labour involved.

Livestock production. Women play a very prominent role in the production and man-agement of livestock; the collection of fodder is also an important activity for them. While men take some responsibility for cattle, women have the most responsibility for small livestock (sheep, goats and chickens).

Reproductive activities. Reproductive activities such as fetching water and fuel, prepar-ing food, carrying food to the farm, child care, washing, and cleaning and decorating the house, are almost exclusively the responsibility of women. Men sometimes help their wives, for instance, when they are ill. Women spend a lot of time collecting drinking water – up to four hours a day in the dry season. The availability of firewood varies, as does the time spent in collecting it.

Seasonal variation. Women's overall workload is highest during the rainy season (between summer and winter), when they have sufficient employment in the village. Work is scarcer during the winter, and scarcest during the summer, when there is little work in the fields and women face many problems. There is a shortage of water for human and animal consumption, a shortage of firewood, fodder and green leaves for human consumption; food becomes a problem. Health problems mostly occur in the summer and at the height of the rainy season. Men migrate mainly during the winter and summer. It may therefore be concluded that summer is the most difficult season for women. The beginning of the rainy season is difficult too: women have to work hard in the fields, but food, fodder and water are still in short supply.

Access to and control over resources

Another aspect of the analysis of gender relations concerns access to and control over various resources and facilities, as well as women's benefits, compared to men.

Productive resources. Few women in the four villages own land themselves. They may inherit it in the absence of male heirs, and in certain cases widows with male children may inherit land to pass on to them. When a woman marries into a landowning family she cultivates this land as a member of the family. Women's access to irrigation is therefore linked to their access to land.

Though women do most of the agricultural labour, men have final control over the produce and its marketing. This does not mean that women have no say over the income derived from produce, but it does mean they are economically dependent on their husbands. Women have some control over revenues from the sale of milk, goats, sheep and chickens. The availability of fodder and grazing land is therefore important to them. The following quotation, from a male farmer in Burgula, shows how agricultural income is divided, as well as the degree of control men and women have over the income and how it is used.

> In vegetable fields, when women weed we watch the fields. After they have plucked the fruit, they fill the bags, and we stitch them up. Then we carry the produce on the bus to Shadnagar, and sell it there on the market. From the money we buy provisions for our household. We have the list of provisions which was given by our wife. We give her the rest of the money, but we keep some for paying back loans and spend some on alcohol.

Women are mainly responsible for providing their household with food. Men are served first and women last. Children under five and women are therefore most at risk of malnutrition. There are some important variations in the food situation between and within the villages studied. In two villages, food availability is an important problem for only the poorest households. In the other two, however, a large part of the population suffers from food insecurity due to the transition to commercial agriculture. Women seem to be better off when they have direct control over the food, as is the case when they are paid in kind, or when they have some control over a product such as milk.

The degree of women's participation in decision-making regarding agriculture and household matters depends both on the resource base of their household and on their 'own' economic resource base: their dowry. Female agricultural labourers get paid in cash, which may give them more control financially than women in farming households. However, this control also brings many worries and heavy responsibility for the survival of their families. In discussing women's scope for decision-making, women in Garlapadu say:

> Women from Reddy households have freedom in taking decisions in agriculture and in the household. This is because their parents give them land and gold as a dowry. Only Reddy women have this privilege. Women in poor families have a say, but even though they think of so many things during their lifetime, still they cannot achieve anything. Single women will go to the market to buy things, they function like the men; the work done by these women is recognized. They take decisions by themselves in agricultural work.

Facilities. In three villages access to drinking-water is a major problem for women, which becomes acute during the summer. Women also complain strongly about the lack of decent bathing and toilet facilities. At the time of the study none of the villages had a health clinic. Hospitals are 20 km or further away. Women say that reproductive health problems and cancers are becoming more frequent. They believe this is related to the increased use of pesticides, which contaminate the food nowadays.

Men regard the *grampanchayat* (village council) as a very important village institution. Village development officers, who coordinate government development programmes at village level, are also regarded as useful and accessible. Women do not mention these officers. For them the school, the shop, the well and the midwife are important and accessible; toilet facilities, however, are important but difficult for them to reach, being on the outskirts of the village.

Small and marginal male farmers regard institutions such as agricultural extension, single window societies (for the provision of agricultural inputs) and banks as far away and not very accessible; for women these institutions are virtually out of the picture. APSIDC is more accessible to men, but not to women. Money lenders are near at hand and easily accessible to men. This, however, is not the case for women, unless they have gold to pawn. Women's awareness of services such as extension and credit facilities is generally low. Many social barriers hinder their access to such facilities. Mobility is a particular problem. A number of single women with no other alternative are prepared to face the problems attached to overcoming such barriers. Many women, however, consider them prohibitive.

Women's self-image. Our impression of women's self-image was mixed. On the one hand they accept things as they are. They realize perfectly well that as women they are valued less than men: 'A boy is born for ten paise, a girl for five, that's how it is.' On the other hand, women can be very articulate about their situation and the desire to change it. This gave us the impression that little outside support would be needed to help them make a real breakthrough in building up their self-confidence. The following quotations selected from the interviews we held with women from different backgrounds support this impression.

Women on self-confidence: 'Women have no self-confidence. This was caused by society, and in particular by men. They promote the belief that women lack intelligence, and that their memory is weak. They don't give any importance or recognition to our thoughts or plans.'

Single women about themselves: 'We have to be very careful, because we are both single and women. When we wear good clothes they can't stand it. When you have a husband you can do some things. But the single woman can't even comb her hair. We can't get married again, especially if we have children. We have to leave the children with our mothers. No mother can put up with a situation like this.'

Women's organizational initiatives. Though women in all the villages take organizational initiatives, they are very informal in character. In Chityal, female agricultural labourers have gravitated naturally into groups which work under contract. The women are interested in undertaking joint activities but feel they need guidance. Single women in particular show a keen interest in getting themselves organized.

Expectations of planned interventions. Men and women in two villages with planned lift irrigation schemes were asked about their hopes for the future. The beneficiaries have high hopes and expect a better quality of life. Non-beneficiaries however felt left out. Women's expectations of the scheme differed. In Marrikuntapalli, a village which still relies mainly on traditional rainfed agriculture, women had great hopes of entering the cash economy. In Garlapadu, where cotton and tobacco are the main crops, women very much wanted to become self-reliant in food and fodder production, with the aid of irrigation.

Gender impact of existing irrigation interventions

In the other two villages selected for the gender assessment study, we analysed the impact on women's position of irrigation interventions that were already in place (a borewell in Burgula, a lift irrigation scheme in Chityal). These had been provided by APSIDC. Since it is difficult if not impossible to isolate this impact from the more general shift of agriculture towards a greater market orientation, it is discussed in the context of general changes in agricultural production relations.

Table 2 presents a comparative picture of the two types of irrigation intervention, and of the changes in Burgula and Chityal due to these interventions. It shows a remarkable difference between the two schemes. Borewells give a small group of beneficiaries a greater sense of security and control. Lift irrigation schemes affect far more people. Besides the type and scale of irrigation intervention, other variables explain why one project gives the beneficiaries greater security and the other produces less security for

Table 2.   Impact of irrigation in Burgula and Chityal: differences between borewells and lift irrigation (LIS)

	Burgula borewell	Chityal LIS
command area	7.5 acres	450 acres*
number of beneficiaries	5 families	about 150 households
changes in cropping pattern	becomes more varied: mix of cash + food crops	less varied: monocropping of paddy rice and groundnut
security of beneficiaries	sufficient irrigation throughout year gives strong sense of security	security depends on water supply; often insufficient; greater social tensions in the village
security of non-beneficiaries	marginal or no impact	less food security, greater social tensions
changes in workload: beneficiaries	women especially get more work in agriculture	women get more work in agriculture
changes in workload: non-beneficiaries	marginal or no impact	women get more work; have little time for domestic activities
employment generation	self-employment of beneficiaries, little additional employment	considerable employment generation, especially for women

* The total scheme of about 3,000 acres covers four villages. Schemes under the APLIFT project will have a maximum size of 1,000 acres

non-beneficiaries and social instability in the village as a whole. For example, Burgula had already been through a process of intensive agricultural change, and has relatively easy access to agricultural services, information and marketing facilities. Chityal has not been through this process, and its access to facilities and information is poor. Moreover there are vested interests at work which accentuate the 'destabilizing' effect of irrigation. Nevertheless, in both types of intervention a positive impact in terms of increased agricultural production, income and employment was observed. There are however a number of negative side effects, which impact women in particular.

In Chityal there is social tension between beneficiaries and non-beneficiaries. Economic inequity is increasing because only a part of the community benefits from irrigation facilities. Families previously on the same economic and social level now occupy different positions in village society. Borewell irrigation creates no such tension, because the intervention is on a much smaller scale. In both villages there is a greater tendency to leave dry land fallow. Small farmers who own only dry land prefer working as wage labourers to eking out a precarious existence on their marginalized lands. The households mainly affected are those where women play a major role in agriculture because men migrate for shorter or longer periods. This tendency to leave dry land fallow will increase with irrigation. It will also lead to greater differentiation between farmers with and without access to irrigation water.

With irrigation, there is a shift from coarse grains to rice as the major staple food. Women say this is very important for them: it is less work. In Chityal, however, this shift also has implications for food security. Coarse grains and pulses are now in short supply. Grain, mainly rice, is sold for cash at a high price, which many people can barely afford. The increasing monotony of the villagers' diet also has negative nutritional consequences.

In Burgula both the quality and quantity of women's work has changed, partly as a consequence of irrigation, partly due to other factors. In the past food processing was far more work for women: grinding millet and sorghum, churning milk, etc. Now this work has been reduced, thanks to facilities such as grinding mills and milk chilling centres. At the same time, irrigation has increased women's work in agriculture. Before irrigation they had one cropping season; now they have two or even three. There are more crops to be looked after, and higher yields bring more post-harvest activities. The cultivation of vegetables in particular means much more work for women. Even so, women preferred working on their own land to going out to work as wage labour. We also noted that, despite a distinct division of labour, the irrigated farms in the borewell scheme are a real family undertaking where men and women work side by side.

In Chityal the advent of irrigation has changed the nature of the work of women labourers and, possibly, of women in beneficiary households. A few years ago, before the lift irrigation scheme started operating, women did not have to go out of the village to work. Now that areas in neighbouring villages are being irrigated, there is more work outside Chityal. While this increases the family income, it also means women have to spend more time and energy walking to and from the fields.

In the past women started work early (by 8 a.m.) and came home for lunch; now they work in the fields from 10 a.m. to 5 p.m. with a short break. If they go out to work in another village, it is even more difficult for them to feed small babies left in the care of others at home. As the women themselves said 'You go out to work and kill your children.' Unless they have a cow or buffalo at home, and can use the milk for the babies, the children simply have to starve. The increasing amount of work in the fields has led to a situation where women do not have enough time or energy for their domestic chores, their children or themselves. This was evident from the state of the younger children as well as the women. The burden of domestic chores is now increasingly shifted to older children, especially girls, and older women. We found only a small number of girls among the few children who did attend school.

Though more work is available the women labourers in Chityal feel insecure. People from surrounding villages are also competing for work. Women who were previously part of a subsistence economy now belong to an organized labour force. This transition has created its own psychological stresses. The dominant work pattern has also changed in the sense that women are now employed in groups whose terms are negotiated by a head-woman or *maistri* (a small contractor who works along with the group). These groups compete for contracts in the command area. Thus the women now have to be careful to maintain proper relations within the work group as well as with the *maistri*. Furthermore, they are never sure where or when they will be working in any given period (sometimes they have to walk from seven to eight kilometres to work). Perhaps the strenuousness of their work has led to the current situation, in which most women labourers drink every day.

When attempting to assess the impact of irrigation on women's workload, a distinction must be made between two categories: group A – women from small and marginal farm households with access to irrigation; and group B – women from the households of marginal farmers and agricultural labourers without access to irrigation. The women in group A will benefit: they will no longer have to go out to work, and their households will definitely become more prosperous. These positive effects outweigh the negative one of becoming financially more dependent on their husbands. The degree of benefit for women in group B depends on the specific situation in the village. Some important factors are:

- the effects of the shift in cropping patterns and shift from income in kind to income in cash on women's household food security and health;
- the increase or decrease in the distance from home to work;
- how the local labour market is affected by the lift irrigation scheme, and the direct consequences for women labourers in terms of wages, competition, working conditions, migration of husbands, etc.

Gender impact of irrigation interventions

Some major conclusions may be drawn from the project, institutional, context and gender analyses conducted in the four villages, and from the assessment of the effects of existing irrigation interventions on the position of women. The first conclusion concerns the project designs. Although the projects' objectives refer explicitly to women farmers as the main beneficiaries, the project designs lack a gender focus. There is no indication of specific outputs and activities, and no specific inputs and budget allocations have been made. We believe that unless a systematic effort is made to incorporate a clear gender focus in the overall project designs (including a proper budget), the interventions cannot be expected to have a significant positive impact on women's position. APLIFT in particular could have a detrimental effect on women (and men) in non-beneficiary households if no steps are taken to counteract unwelcome side effects. Secondly, the institutional analysis suggests that neither project has a policy on a gender-sensitive approach. It is not clear how the future implementing institutions are supposed to develop such an approach. Neither the specific roles and tasks regarding this aspect nor the expertise required are explicitly mentioned in the documents. Thirdly, the context analysis shows that the process of change in agricultural production in Andhra Pradesh affects women and men differently. For small and marginal farm households, for example, it implies:

- a shift in the gender division of labour, due to the transition from a traditional mixed cropping pattern to a pattern emphasizing the monocropping of cash crops. Women remain in charge of 'traditional' food crops and men take responsibility for 'modern' cash crops;
- a shift in control over production towards men, due to a shift from a strongly

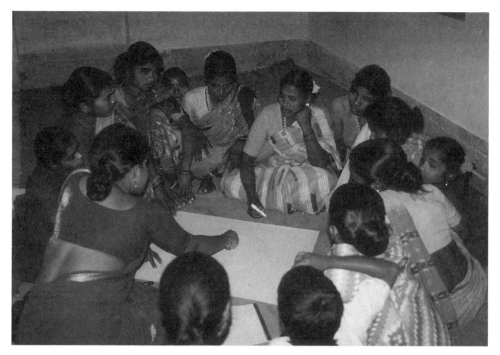

Venn diagram exercise being carried out with a small homogeneous group of women
(Photo: Annet Lingen)

subsistence oriented economy towards integration in the market economy. Women complain that, because of commercial crops, agriculture is being taken away from them. Men go for bank loans, buy seeds, and purchase pesticides and fertilizers. They buy hybrid variety seeds of sorghum and *bajra* (millet) which, like the traditional varieties, do give good fodder. Women do the bulk of the agricultural labour at home. They still have control over minor crops such as *jowar* (sorghum), legumes, etc. But commercialization prevents them from interacting with men, and men are unable to share their experiences with women;

- a shift from payment of wages in kind to payment in cash, affecting the food security of the households of agricultural labourers. The money earned is not enough to buy the equivalent of what they used to get in kind, which was sufficient to feed the family for that day;
- more work for female labourers in agriculture. Men, however, migrate increasingly to other areas for work;
- increased use of pesticides, which may affect the health of women more than men.

Fourthly, the gender analysis at microlevel gives due weight to the nuances of the major trends observable in agricultural production in general. The pilot study does show that the gender impact of irrigation interventions depends largely on contextual variables. It also shows that it is important to take such variables into account when designing and implementing a specific irrigation intervention.

An examination of the effects of the two existing irrigation schemes allows a fifth group of conclusions. We observed that – within the overall context of modernization of agriculture – a specific irrigation intervention can have very different effects. It can *reinforce* the negative impact of agricultural change: the process of change, as outlined above, is speeded up in a rather uncontrolled manner. This was observed in Chityal, which quite suddenly switched from a subsistence oriented economy to a cash economy after the installation of a lift irrigation scheme. An irrigation intervention can also help to *balance* such negative effects. Burgula, for example, is a village which already had many private irrigation facilities, but small and marginal farm households had no access to irrigation. The installation by APSIDC of a borewell two years ago gave these households access to irrigation, which reduced differences between them and other farm households.

The gender impact in the two villages with existing schemes is also quite different, the crucial factor being the scale of the intervention. With a borewell, just a few households are the intended beneficiaries; a lift irrigation scheme, however, directly affects several hundred households and indirectly a whole village, sometimes several villages.

In Burgula (borewell) the irrigation intervention has mainly led to increased self-employment and an increased sense of security among women from beneficiary households. In Chityal (lift irrigation) there was a similar effect on beneficiaries, but the impact on women from non-beneficiary households was quite negative. These women are more frequently confronted with food security problems at home and an increasing workload as labourers, as well as increased social tensions within their households and in the community. And the heavier workload of adolescent girls prevents them from going go school.

The observed difference in gender impact has implications for the specific approaches to be taken in borewell and lift schemes. Lift irrigation schemes, for example, require a carefully designed strategy to anticipate negative effects, especially on women from non-beneficiary households. These women, for instance, feel a need for home gardens; the projects could examine the feasibility of setting up a home gardening programme to prevent further deterioration of their nutritional situation.

The last conclusion concerns the methodology of the gender assessment study. The context and gender analyses in particular illustrate the danger of assuming 'the target group' is homogeneous, not only in terms of gender but in sociocultural terms as well. Therefore it is necessary to separate a project's targeted population group into relevant socioeconomic categories, taking ethnic and cultural differences into account. The pilot study made the following differentiation: a) small farm households which can in principle live on the revenues from their own land; b) small and marginal farm households dependent to a varying degree on income from agricultural labour or migration; and c) landless agricultural labourers completely dependent on their income from labour. An important characteristic of the last two categories is that women play a crucial role in farming activities, because their husbands often migrate in search of work.

The analyses also make clear that it is difficult to predict who will gain from a project intervention, even when the target group is clearly defined in the project documents. The projects are targeted at small and marginal male and female farmers who are supposed to benefit from the irrigation facilities provided. Access to these facilities is strongly connected with access to land. The study clearly reveals that the degree of benefit landowning households derive from irrigation provisions depends on whether their income derives from their land and/or agricultural labour (mainly women), or from work elsewhere (mostly men). Moreover, the irrigation interventions are likely to affect other groups in the area: small and marginal farmers and agricultural labourers with no land in the command area of the projects.

In other words, it is important to differentiate these various categories, to discover who is likely to benefit and under which conditions. Proper insight into the various effects of a project intervention obviously has implications for the strategies proposed.

To summarize, regarding the (expected) gender impact of the irrigation interventions of APWELL and APLIFT on women and gender relations we can say that:
- Women in small farm households able in principle to live on the revenues from their own land will benefit. Their workload may increase, but an improved socioeconomic position will enable them to hire labourers to help with some of the work.
- Some small and marginal households dependent to a varying extent on income derived from agricultural labour or migration will get access to enough irrigation water to meet their needs. Women in these households will benefit. They will no longer work as agricultural labour, and the prosperity of their households will increase. All this outweighs the negative effect of becoming financially more dependent on their husbands.
- Women in these beneficiary households are most likely to gain in terms of nutrition, health, and self-image. They may lose in terms of participation in decision-making. Their household income will increase, but they will have less control over it.
- Other small and marginal households dependent on agricultural labour/migration will get no access to irrigation, or insufficient for their needs. Women in these households will benefit less or not at all, or will experience negative effects. The same applies to women from landless households totally dependent on income from labour. The type of impact they experience depends on a number of contextual variables which have already been discussed.
- Women from non-beneficiary households in villages with lift irrigation schemes may lose out in terms of nutrition, health, means of production, self-image and workload. They may gain in terms of employment. Their income may increase because there is more work; on the other hand their cash income will buy less food per day than they used to get in kind before the scheme started.
- Women in non-beneficiary households in villages with borewell schemes may in certain cases experience a decreasing water table in their local drinking-water wells. Otherwise there will be no significant effect.

Proposal for a gender-specific strategy

The projects do have some scope for anticipating the negative effects observed. However, a systematic effort must be made to design a gender-specific strategy which actually addresses the issues in question. Based on the conclusions of the gender assessment study, a gender strategy related to activities at the various stages of scheme implementation is suggested here. Such a strategy will not be effective, however, unless it meets certain requirements: firstly, a programme of activities must be developed gradually. A sound institutional framework needs to be worked out to allow smooth collaboration between APSIDC, NGOs and the other institutions to be involved. The projects' technical and social components need to be properly matched. The implementation schedule for NGO activities needs adjusting to what is practicable: effectively involving women in the projects will take time. Much is required of the staff of the NGOs, which will need the support of the Programme Support Office. It should be clear by now that gender expertise ought to be included in the Support Office and in the NGO component of the project. Collaboration between APSIDC and NGOs will be effective if it focuses on concrete activities in which each party has a clear role to play.

Secondly, the budget should be adjusted to include the human resources and material inputs needed to operationalize the gender component. Thirdly, the gender component must be closely monitored: the gender assessment study shows that, without a coherent gender strategy, negative effects are likely. Different sets of indicators must be developed for the two projects. A key concern of APLIFT is to monitor the project's impact on female agricultural labourers (particularly in terms of workload and nutrition). For the APWELL project, it is more important to monitor the impact on women in the various beneficiary households (focusing on women's control of various aspects of agricultural production). Among the indicators that could be used are women's workload and gender division of labour; women's access to and control over income; women's access to irrigated land; the extent of male and female migration from and to the village; the formation and existence of women's groups/organizations; women's access to institutions (especially banks and agricultural extension); the nutritional state of women and children; and the use of pesticides, and their effects on health.

With these requirements in mind, APSIDC and NGOs could jointly undertake the following activities at project level, during each implementation phase:

1. At the initiation stage target farmers (beneficiaries) should be identified, in accord with the criteria set in the project document. At this stage it is important to identify marginal farm households managed by women (for part of the year or permanently). Ways of involving various categories of women in the project must be carefully examined: a distinction must be made between women from households with access to irrigation, and women outside this category who could be involved in other ways (for example, as construction labourers or as village mechanics).

2. APSIDC and NGO field staff in newly identified schemes should undertake a joint baseline study, to identify priority target groups and relevant village level institutions. Baseline information should be collected on village socioeconomic profiles, cropping patterns, gender division of labour, household economy, access to institutions, priority needs of women and men, and existing village level institutions. The approach and methodology could be similar to that of the RRAs which took place in the context of the gender assessment study (see Chapter 1).

3. APSIDC and NGOs should jointly assess the crops that farmers (men and women) want to grow under the scheme, since this could have implications for the design. Food security must be an important consideration. In the case of APLIFT irrigation, some water must be provided for growing food (paddy rice and vegetables) for home consumption, as well as for fodder crops.

4. Sufficient time must be allowed for building up the effective participation of women – at least one year before construction starts: women's participation in irrigation projects does not happen automatically; it must be facilitated. An important first step will be to form women's groups (or strengthen existing groups). It is important to organize such groups around specific activities of direct and practical interest to the women involved: examples are irrigation, or something like saving and credit or functional literacy. Such groups can help women to build up the self-confidence and strength they need to effectively handle the challenges posed by the irrigation project. Women from landowning households may have different interests and priorities from landless women. Separate functional groups may be necessary. NGOs could support the formation of such groups, or liaise with other persons and organizations. It is important to identify any existing informal institutions that could form a basis for the further organization of women.

5. During the construction stage, farmers/women's organizations should be used to recruit labour; they could be given a group contract.

6. At the initial operational stage, APSIDC field staff, together with the NGO staff, should decide who should be trained in operation and maintenance; they should also consider the feasibility of involving women in such a training programme. Village women recommended a policy of reserving 50 per cent of the jobs (as *laskars* – irrigation field workers, and other water management jobs) in the lift irrigation schemes for women.

7. At the operational stage attention will be paid to privatizing the schemes. An operational strategy must be developed to encourage the households managed by women (part-time or full time) to participate. Such a strategy should include the following elements:
   – information on the irrigation schemes, loan facilities etc. disseminated directly to women;
   – credit facilities that are really accessible to these women;
   – feasible and practical agricultural extension packages for women, which make allowances for the labour and financial constraints of women, and their preferences and priorities (food security, provision of fodder and other household needs);
   – clear priorities regarding who is to benefit from the projects' special loan fund, which has a comparatively limited capacity. Priority should be given to farm households managed by women;
   – the establishment of a simple system of consumer credit especially targeted at women should be considered: they are strongly affected by the shift from a personal daily wage to a farm household income.

Summary

This proposal for a gender-specific strategy is based on the results of the gender assessment study carried out in India. It illustrates the way such a study can contribute to better project planning, by suggesting ways to take the expected effects of project interventions on gender relations into consideration. The gender assessment study, with its four interrelated analyses, collected information that is essential for the effective realization of project objectives. The methodological structure of interrelated analyses facilitated the collection of information on gender relations in the project area, within the general context of agricultural development in India. This structure also made possible an assessment of the strengths and weaknesses of the projects, including their institutional setting, from a gender perspective.

Note

1. The pilot gender assessment study in India was carried out from January to March 1993. ETC Foundation (ETC-F), a consultancy group based in the Netherlands, was contracted for the study in India. ETC-India, a branch of ETC-F, subcontracted the Indian consultancy group Think Soft for the preparatory study and the implementation of the fieldwork, in collaboration with the Dutch ETC consultant.

Bibliography

Agarwal, B. (1986) Women, poverty and agricultural growth in India. In: Journal of Peasant Studies, 13 (4) pp. 165–220.

Kumari, R. (1991) Women-headed households in rural India. Radiant Publishers, New Delhi.

Lalita K. and K.S. Gopal (1993) Briefing paper on gender impact study. Prepared for M/S Think Soft, Hyderabad.

Mies, M., Lalita K. and K. Kumari (1984) Indian women in subsistence and agricultural labour. International Labour Office, Geneva.

Royal Netherlands Embassy (1990) Women in the Netherlands' assisted irrigation projects. New Delhi.

Sharma, U. (1980) Women, work and property in North West India. London, Tavistock Publications.

Walsum, E.M. van, et al. (1993a) Gender impact study in the Andhra Pradesh Surface Water Lift Irrigation Schemes and Groundwater Borewell Irrigation Schemes, a pilot study in India. ETC, Leusden.

Walsum, E.M. van, et al. (1993b) Gender impact study in the Andhra Pradesh Surface Water Lift Irrigation Schemes and Borewell Irrigation Schemes, report on the Methodology. ETC. Leusden.

World Bank (1991) Gender and poverty in India. A World Bank country study, Washington.

5

Conclusions

A gender assessment study investigates the expected impact of a project on women and assesses whether, and to what extent, the project responds to the specific interests and needs of various categories of women, as compared to men. Moreover, it provides relevant general information for further project planning, in that it identifies activities that are apt to be particularly relevant to women. This chapter discusses the methodology and results of three gender assessment studies, as well as the scope of the three related development projects to improve women's position. Some recommendations are given for increasing the effectiveness of gender assessment studies and project interventions.

Combination of analyses

The great strength of a gender assessment study is its four-component analytical structure: the context analysis, project analysis, institutional analysis and gender analysis at microlevel. Each component must be regarded as related to the others. This combination of interrelated analyses also enables a gender assessment to address the strengths and weaknesses of a project proposal that, in a strict sense, go beyond gender issues.

Another strong element of a gender assessment study is its clear target group focus: the methodology includes mechanisms for reaching the target group, and the implementation of the study's recommendations is intended primarily to improve the project proposal regarding the needs of the women concerned.

Relation between the context and gender analyses

The general context, or space in which men, women and groups operate, inevitably influences the situation at household and community level. Thus, the context analysis, which incorporates economic, political, social and cultural aspects, gives insight into the broader macro setting of the project. It describes the setting in which developments at the microlevel (where the project intends to make an impact) take place. The gender analysis, which is carried out during fieldwork in the villages, explores the situation at microlevel. It assesses the possibilities and limitations set by the roles and activities of men and women, their varying degrees of access to and control over resources, benefits and institutions, their self-image and confidence, and their organizational capacities.

In the case studies the context analysis took place before the gender analysis at microlevel and thus provided a critical input to the field study. The emphasis put on the family and the communal organization in the gender analysis in Bolivia, for instance, was based on knowledge of specific socioeconomic and cultural aspects of Andean peasant society.

The importance of the interrelationship between the macro and microlevel can be seen in the impact on men and women of general changes taking place in the agricultural production process. In Bolivia and India, for example, a shift was observed from a traditional mixed cropping pattern towards a monocropping production system that emphasizes market integration. In Bolivia, promotion of commercial crop production by various development organizations (governmental and non-governmental) is focused on men. Men participate in producers' associations where they can obtain seed, fertilizer, credit, etc. Women, however, are increasingly excluded from decisions which they used to take about production. In India, the observed change has led to a shift in control over production from women to men; women remain in charge of the 'traditional' food crops while men take responsibility for the 'modern' cash crops. Men obtain bank loans, buy seeds, purchase pesticides and fertilizers. Women in both Bolivia and India complain that control over production is being taken away from them.

Analysis of the project proposal
In general, a project proposal should strive to integrate developments at macro and microlevel in a society, as a basis for its formulation of relevant and realistic objectives, strategies, interventions and plans. Assumptions underlying the design of interventions, as well as the expected output and benefits, should be critically examined. The project analysis gives insight into the coherence and feasibility of the project proposal and checks its internal consistency: it looks at the way gender issues are addressed in objectives, assumptions, strategies, etc. Thus, it increases insight into the strengths and weaknesses of the project with regard to its gender perspective and approach.

The analyses of the proposals in the three pilot studies showed insufficient critical consideration of the general socioeconomic and cultural context, in particular the factors influencing gender relations. It also appeared that none of the proposals is based on a gender-specific needs assessment of the beneficiaries. The three proposals are instead based on unverified assumptions about the position of women and gender relations at household and community level, and in society in general. In Burkina Faso, the assumption is that women are mainly involved in reproductive activities, and that female farmers can be addressed in the same way as male farmers, without analyzing their possibilities for access to resources. In India, the assumption that female heads of household in the target group can claim their right to access to irrigation facilities overlooks the low degree of women's participation in village level decision-making, as well as their low capacity to make claims in general. In Bolivia, it is assumed that the promotion of women's organizations will increase their participation in communal decision-making processes, despite the fact that these groups have already existed in the project area for about 15 years without having had any influence in the public sector.

The degree of consistency among objectives, strategies, proposed activities and desired results varies in the three proposals, especially with regard to gender issues. In Burkina Faso, inconsistency appears at the general level: either the objectives and strategies proposed are not elaborated in activities, or they do not correspond with the activities and the expected outcomes. In India, the attention that is paid to women in the objectives and the general strategies is not operationalized in activities, expected results, etc. In Bolivia, the objectives and strategies are fairly consistent, but the assumptions on which they are based differ from those underlying the proposed activities.

Analysis of the institutional setting

The project proposal analysis is closely linked with the institutional analysis, which gives a picture of the institutional setting for the project. This analysis examines the policy and perceptions – regarding gender relations – of the implementing institutions, as well as their capacities for planning, implementation and cooperation.

The implementing institutions in the case studies have varying degrees of institutional capacity. In Bolivia, the implementing institution has a sound women and development policy plus the organizational capacity to take this policy seriously. In Burkina Faso and India, various institutions are involved in implementing the proposed projects. The institutional arrangements in India are inconsistent; the various mandates of the government agencies and the participating NGO, and the coordination between them, have not been defined. It is not clear, for instance, why it is automatically assumed that NGOs have the capacity to pay attention to women's position. Nevertheless, the institutions concerned do have a certain awareness of women's role. The institutions involved in the Burkina Faso project show a virtual lack of awareness of this role. In both cases the capacities to plan, coordinate and cooperate at project level is minimal. As a result, only a few isolated concerns regarding women are presented. Clearly, strengths and weaknesses at the institutional level must be taken into account in the project proposal, to promote effective implementation in general and to deal properly with gender issues in particular.

Although the combination of four analyses is the great strength of the gender assessment study, these analyses do not necessarily have to be carried out during a single study period, but could be spread out over time.

Results and recommendations

That a gender assessment study can contribute to a better understanding, and if necessary modification, of a project's approach to gender issues is borne out by the results of the three case studies, brought together in this section.

Main results

All three studies show that access to and control over resources are the most critical issues for small and marginal farm households. If this is very limited or non-existent it is very difficult for small and marginal households to use the proposed project interventions effectively.

The Bolivia study showed that access to and control over land and water are essential to both male and female farmers, while for women access to an additional resource – finance – is very important. In the Burkina Faso study access to extension facilities appeared to be essential for women. Although they have an integrated role in the family farm they are neglected by extension services, thus project interventions will not necessarily reach them. The India study showed that access to irrigation facilities is only relevant if male and female farmers get access to and control over land of sufficient size and quality to earn revenue to live on. Women also need access to labour (family or hired) to help them when husbands migrate in search of work. Evidently access to and control over resources in general are more critical issues for households managed by women; they are not automatically at women's disposal.

Each study also produced specific results concerning the institutional aspects and gender impact of the proposed project interventions. The main points are summarized here.

In Bolivia, the interventions proposed to decrease the number of livestock are based on general environmental considerations. The crucial role women play in livestock production, the fact that livestock is regarded as a 'nest egg' and women's important contribution to the family income through the processing of wool are not taken into consideration. Unless sound alternatives are proposed, a decrease in the number of livestock will have a negative effect on women's economic position within the household.

Proposed interventions to set up women's groups to implement some small-scale productive activities are not supported by proper feasibility studies. Since their economic viability is likely to be limited, these interventions will have a negative impact on women's position in the family and in the community. The proposed activities are derived from women's reproductive tasks and are of marginal economic importance, which will lead to women's increasing exclusion from economic decisions that directly affect them.

The study also concludes that while a sound institutional women and development policy is a necessary condition to ensure that project interventions take women's position and gender relations into account in a specific socioeconomic context, it is not enough on its own. The project interventions are based on often-wrong assumptions about poverty and women's role in peasant society, which are inconsistent with the institutional women and development policy.

In India, the study showed that the implementing institutions lack a sound women and development policy and a clear gender-sensitive approach. Nor is there any indication of how the institutions are supposed to develop such an approach. The conclusion therefore is that the project proposals lack a gender focus.

Regarding the impact of proposed interventions, the following conclusions are drawn. In terms of nutrition, health and self-image, women from beneficiary households will probably gain from the introduction of both lift and borewell irrigation schemes. They may lose in terms of participation in decision-making. Their household income will increase, but their control over this income will decrease.

Women from non-beneficiary households may lose out in terms of nutrition, health, means of production, self-image and workload as a result of lift irrigation schemes. They may, however, gain in terms of employment. Their income may increase because there is more work; on the other hand, their cash income will buy less food per day than they used to get in kind before the scheme started.

The introduction of borewell schemes might affect women in some non-beneficiary households by lowering the water level in their local drinking-water wells. They will not, however, experience any other significant effects.

In Burkina Faso the proposed interventions are mainly concerned with women's reproductive tasks. Other interventions regarding food processing and storage of and trade in agricultural products aim to improve production conditions only, overlooking women's direct role in the agricultural production process. Thus there is a definite risk that women's productive tasks will be marginalized, if not neglected.

If interventions in the field of livestock, agricultural research and extension do not indicate how women will be involved, women will not benefit from them and their position, compared to men, will not improve.

Furthermore, the institutional framework presented in the project proposal is too weak in terms of planning, implementation and coordination capacities to guarantee a viable operation. Consequently, an adequate gender-sensitive approach is unfeasible.

Main recommendations

It is clear that the three projects have different institutional settings with varying degrees of gender awareness. The type of intervention and the expected gender impact also vary according to the contextual variables at micro and macrolevel. Therefore these three gender assessment studies make different recommendations concerning future institutional aspects and proposed activities. Besides the specific recommendations made to the various implementing organizations, which are not presented here,[1] three general recommendations are relevant to this overview.

The Burkina Faso study recommends a total reorientation of objectives and intervention strategies. The India study advises projects to develop a gender-specific strategy that addresses the issues brought forward in the study, and proposes a general outline for a gender strategy. It is clear from both studies that gender issues cannot be incorporated at the same pace everywhere; the institutions involved have different levels of gender awareness, which can lead to friction during the implementation of projects. The Bolivia study advises the implementing organization to make a more detailed workplan, taking the institutional and microlevel gender analyses into account, and makes various suggestions for a workplan that addresses the needs of the women concerned.

Assessing the gender assessment study

The main results of the three case studies presented above lead to some general conclusions about the positive contributions of a gender assessment study, as well as its limitations.

Positive contributions

A gender assessment gives insight into a proposed project's approach to gender, as well as the way gender relations manifest themselves in the project area. It enables project interventions to be assessed for their relevance to women, from a gender perspective. In that sense a gender assessment study contributes to an understanding of the possible impact of proposed project interventions on women and gender relations. Since a gender assessment study usually takes place at the beginning of the project cycle, its conclusions about the expected effects of project interventions are hypothetical. Therefore it could be used to formulate specific questions for further, more detailed research. For example, a question relevant to the project in Bolivia might be: 'what are the potential and the limitations of the women's groups, already in existence for about 15 years, regarding decision-making processes at community level.'

The examination of specific local and cultural characteristics at microlevel gives a clearer picture of the general trends observed at macrolevel. This refinement is necessary to develop strategies for interventions that pay due attention to gender relations and women's position in a certain area.

These remarks suggest that a gender assessment study will lead to improved project formulation and design, adequately integrating a gender strategy. However, to achieve this, the study must not be an isolated exercise. It must be followed up to ensure accurate incorporation of gender concerns in implementation and evaluation. In this sense, a gender assessment study may be regarded as an ongoing analytical process which can also be used at various stages, such as project formulation, the elaboration of concrete workplans and the implementation of activities, as well as for monitoring and evaluation. Certain components could be repeated during the implementation of the project to monitor the effectiveness of strategies and make any necessary adjustments.

Limitations

Despite its positive contributions to project formulation and design, a gender assessment study – as defined for the pilot studies – has its limitations. For one thing it is a relatively time-consuming and costly exercise, which should be used with careful consideration. Moreover, it requires specialized expertise to combine the components of a gender assessment in a way that achieves a good interrelation between the macro and microanalyses. The most important limitation, however, concerns the risk of unduly raising the expectations of the population involved in the gender analysis at microlevel. Since a gender assessment study takes place early in the project cycle, it is often not yet clear whether the people who are being asked to devote time and energy to the analyses will benefit from any project interventions. This aspect must not be carelessly overlooked.

Critical conditions to be met

A number of preconditions must be met if the potential effectiveness of a gender assessment study is to be realized. A first requirement is institutional soundness: the capacity of institutions to implement a project. A second requirement of the staff of implementing institutions is readiness to modify the project approach, particularly in terms of gender. This attitude is even more important than skills and capacities in the field of gender. Training can help to develop such skills if staff are willing to discuss gender aspects and the incorporation of a gender perspective in project approach and methods (including monitoring). It is advisable to make allowances for the different levels of knowledge of gender issues within the institutions, as well as for the varying degrees of staff commitment to gender-sensitive policies and implementation strategies. A last requirement is consistency of project objectives, strategies, activities and outcomes. All three studies show clearly that it is not enough to mention women in objectives and/or in policies: operationalization is essential.

The authors recommend a pre-study to find out whether these requirements are adequately met. This pre-study could consist of a project analysis and an institutional analysis in the first instance, followed by a context analysis to gain insight into the possible effectiveness of a gender assessment study. Going on to conduct a field study is only useful when this can be expected to provide a positive contribution – that is, to add information to the gender assessment study.

Gender relations

A final consideration is the nature of the gender assessment study. The case studies presented here put more emphasis on women and their situation than on the relations between men and women. However, the authors believe that a focus on gender relations is essential if the position of women is to be adequately addressed. Thus, the approach should be refined, adding techniques to include gender relations in a wider sense. Image and self-image, for instance, should refer to women's perception of themselves and their view of men, as well as to men's perception of themselves and their view of women. The objectives, strategies, and other element of the project analysis should be assessed to see how they address women's position and how they deal with the relations between men and women. Such a gender oriented approach will result in better and more realistic insight into the way relations between women and men are shaped in a particular society, and into the impact of project interventions on the position of women as compared to men.

Note

1. These recommendations, while too project-specific to summarize here, can be found in the various reports mentioned in note 2 of the Introduction.

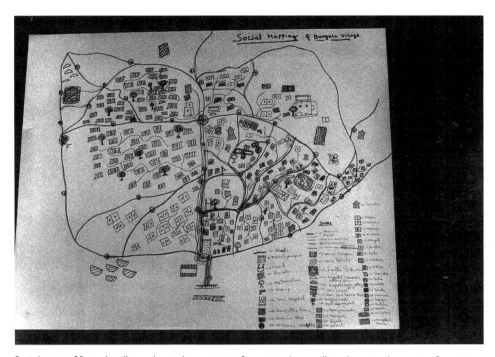

Social map of Burgula village, drawn by a group of women: shows village layout, where specific castes live, and contact of village areas with services (nurse, NGO, revenue officer, and so forth)

(Photo: Annet Lingen)

About the authors

Vera Gianotten trained as an anthropologist and sociologist; her PhD. is in rural sociology. She has worked in Latin America for fourteen years and has, since 1989, been a senior researcher in the Department of Agriculture and Enterprise Development within the Royal Tropical Institute in Amsterdam. She has published a variety of books and articles on her research. The research projects in which she is currently involved include gender analysis of development interventions, participatory approaches to the identification, formulation and evaluation of development interventions, the role of NGOs in the development of civil society, and the cultural dimensions of development.

Verona Groverman, a rural sociologist, has built up her experience with gender issues in rural development through her work both in universities and in the field, including projects in Africa that use a participatory approach. For a number of years she has worked as a consultant in rural and agricultural development, specializing in gender issues, primarily in Africa and Asia. Her tasks include technical assistance and evaluation, as well as training. At present, she is with ETC International BV (consultants in development programmes) in the Netherlands.

Edith van Walsum's university background is in rural development sociology, extension and nutrition. She has worked with governmental and non-governmental organizations in West Africa and Sri Lanka. Her extensive experience with gender issues in agriculture has included both her work as assistant professor in the Department of Gender Studies in Agriculture at Wageningen Agricultural University and that as a consultant in Africa and Asia. She currently works for ETC International BV as a teamleader for a project focused on sustainable agriculture in South India.

Lida Zuidberg is a rural sociologist who specializes in household studies. She has worked in Indonesia and Mali as well as the Netherlands, and at present is a consultant within the Department of Agriculture and Enterprise Development of the Royal Tropical Institute, Amsterdam. Her focus is on participatory research and extension methods, including gender analysis, as a part of technical assistance to agricultural and primary health care projects in West and East Africa.